My
LIFE
in
LEADERSHIP

The Journey and Lessons
Learned Along the Way

FRANCES HESSELBEIN

Foreword by Jim Collins

JOSSEY-BASS
A Wiley Imprint
www.josseybass.com

Published by Jossey-Bass
A Wiley Imprint
989 Market Street, San Francisco, CA 94103-1741—www.josseybass.com

Library of Congress Cataloging-in-Publication Data

Hesselbein, Frances.
   My Life in Leadership: The Journey and Lessons Learned Along the Way / Frances Hesselbein; foreword by Jim Collins.
     p. cm.
   Includes index.
   ISBN 978-0-470-90573-9
   1. Hesselbein, Frances. Women chief executive officers—United States—Biography. 3. Girl Scouts of the United States of America—Management. 4. Peter F. Drucker Foundation for Nonprofit Management. 5. Leadership. I. Title.
   HC102.5.H47A3 2011
   658.0092 – dc22
   [B]   2010045733

Printed in the United States of America
FIRST EDITION
HB Printing   10 9 8 7 6 5 4 3 2 1

CONTENTS

I am deeply grateful to all who have helped me on my journey. Many are noted in the pages that follow, but there are far more who have blessed my life whom I could not recognize in this account (including the countless young people I meet on campuses and academies across the nations, who always give me new energy and new hope). This book is dedicated to all of them, whether named or not, around the world. They are our future.

This book also is dedicated to the men and women in uniform, past, present, and future, whose selfless service has sustained the democracy since the beginning of our country. My father, my husband, my brother, and my son John are part of this sturdy band. They are an inspiration to us all and teach us that service is a privilege, a remarkable opportunity. To serve is to live.

FOREWORD

In October of 2007, I sat with Frances Hesselbein in an enclosed conference room — no windows, maps on the wall, literally bombproof. We'd come together to spend time with the general officers of the 82nd Airborne at Fort Bragg, North Carolina. At the other end of the table sat the commander, General Lloyd J. Austin III, six-foot-four, a muscular two-hundred-plus pounds, winner of a Silver Star for gallantry in combat, responsible for thirty-five thousand soldiers, the power of the man amplified by his calm and quiet. On either side of Austin sat about a dozen one- and two-star generals, along with some colonels, in Army fatigues, all with on-the-ground experience in places like Iraq and Afghanistan.

General Austin had thought hard about this day, part of a final "get ready" time before his command redeployed to Iraq. This was their third deployment to that country. He wanted something special to inspire his general officers as they left their families once again, in service. His dream: a visit and leadership session from Frances Hesselbein. General Austin called and asked if I would come to Fort Bragg and engage Frances in a conversation with the generals.

General Austin began the meeting, "We are so fortunate to have with us one of the great leaders in America, Frances

Hesselbein." The Army generals hushed, and I began to ask Frances questions about leadership, based on her experiences leading the Girl Scouts of the USA back to greatness, earning her a spot on the cover of *Business Week* as America's best manager. Here sat gruff and rumble general officers who'd chosen to jump out of airplanes and lead combat battalions as a career, men who carry personal responsibility for the lives of thousands of young men and women. In business, failed leadership loses money; in the military, failed leadership loses lives.

As Frances talked, the generals sat utterly riveted, for two full hours. Diminutive, no more than five-foot-two, she held a commanding presence like Yoda dispensing wisdom to a gathering of Jedi knights. At the end of her session, the general officers spontaneously shouted *Hooah!*

It matters not the group—Fortune 500 CEOs, philanthropists, college students, social sector leaders, or military general officers in a war zone—Frances has the same effect on people. She inspires and teaches, not just because of what she says, but because of who she is. Leadership, she teaches, begins not with what you do, but with who you *are*. What are your values? What do you serve? What makes you get up every day and bring positive, go-forward tilt to everything and everyone you touch? She believes to her core the U.S. Army idea of "Be - Know - Do." Because we cannot predict what challenges we will face, the most important preparation for leadership lies in developing personal character; you can learn the rest along the way.

In this book, Hesselbein shares her own story, her own life journey into a person of character. She describes the forces that shaped her, including a family that instilled in her the belief that "to serve is to live." Like many great leaders, she did not choose her responsibilities. When her father died, she returned home from school and assumed responsibility for the family. Later in life, she led a Girl Scout council in Johnstown, Pennsylvania. A couple of members of the local council took her to lunch one day, and one of them said, "We've found the perfect leader to be our new executive director of the Talus Rock Girl Scout Council."

"Oh, that's wonderful," exclaimed Frances. "Who?"

"You, Frances."

"But I am a volunteer, not really prepared for this," she replied.

"We think you are the right person," they pressed.

"OK," she finally relented, "I'll do this for six months while we look for a *real* leader."

Six years later, she would leave Pennsylvania to become the CEO of the Girl Scouts of the USA. She would hold the position for thirteen years, the first chief executive to come from the field in sixty-four years, and would lead a great turnaround. The Girl Scouts of the USA faced eight straight years of declining membership and turned to Frances to reverse the slide. In taking the role, she never thought of herself as being "on top" of the organization, but in service to a cause larger than herself. One of her greatest accomplishments came in leading the Girl Scouts to become a place where girls of all origins, whether black, white, Latina, American Indian, or Eskimo, and any form of immigrant, regardless of race or culture, could find themselves. Under her leadership, the Girl Scouts regained momentum, reaching a membership of 2.25 million girls with a workforce (mainly volunteers) of 780,000. Equally important, she set up the organization to be successful beyond her, with an ever increasing size and diversity of members and volunteers.

After the Girl Scouts, Frances became the founding president and CEO of the Peter F. Drucker Foundation for Nonprofit Management, now the Leader to Leader Institute, inspired by her friend and mentor Peter Drucker. She has spent the last two decades multiplying her leadership three-fold: her own leadership example multiplied by teaching leadership to others multiplied by leading an organization dedicated to inspired leadership in the business and social sectors. In all my years of working with leaders, from nonprofits to Fortune 500 companies, from government executives to philanthropists, from military leaders to school principals, I have met not a single person who has had a larger multiplicative effect than Frances. In recognition of her extraordinary multiplicative contributions, she received the Presidential Medal of Freedom, the United States of America's highest civilian honor, in 1998.

I believe that people exude either "positive valence" or "negative valence." Positive-valence people increase the energy in the room every time they enter. Frances has been for me a "double positive valence"—adding energy every time I have the chance to be with her. It's like plugging into a human power source.

During one of our long conversations, I asked Frances how she endured the burdens of leadership and sustained her energy.

"Burden?" She looked puzzled. "Burden? Oh no, leadership is never a burden; it is a privilege."

"But how do you sustain the energy for leadership? We all have limits, but I've never seen you reach yours."

"Everything I have been called to do *gives* me energy. The greater the call, the greater the energy; it comes from outside me."

And perhaps that is one of the great secrets of leadership that Frances teaches with her life. If you are open to being called, if you see service not as a cost to your life but as life itself, then you cannot help but be caught in a giant self-reinforcing circle. You are called to leadership, and your energy rises to the call, you then lead effectively and are called to greater responsibility, your energy rises again to the call, and so it goes. The late John Gardner (author of the classic book *Self-Renewal* and founder of Common Cause) taught me that one absolute requirement for leadership is an extraordinarily high energy level. Frances taught me that one of the greatest sources of energy is leadership done in the spirit of service.

It is no surprise, then, that in 2009, one of our greatest leadership training grounds, the U.S. Military Academy at West Point, made Frances Hesselbein the Class of 1951 Chair for the Study of Leadership. I'm certain that General Austin, himself a West Point graduate, feels that the cadets have been blessed by a great stroke of good fortune to have Frances as a teacher and mentor. I picture her sitting with these young leaders, a walking exemplar of the West Point "Be - Know - Do" philosophy, modeling the Big Lesson: no matter what knocks you down, you get up and go forward. You might be appalled by horrifying events, but never discouraged. You might need to deal with mean-spirited and petty people along the way, but never lose your own gracious manner. You might need to confront a litany of brutal facts and destabilizing uncertainties, but it is your responsibility, as a leader, to always shine a light.

Jim Collins
Boulder, Colorado
December 2010

INTRODUCTION:
BEING CALLED FORWARD

On January 15, 1998, I was at the White House, seated in the East Room, to receive our country's highest civilian award, the Presidential Medal of Freedom. I was overwhelmed that day—and I am still overwhelmed. In the front row before a low stage, I sat with other honorees, including David Rockefeller, Admiral Zumwalt, Brooke Astor, James Farmer, and Dr. Robert Coles. Each of us had a military aide to escort us to the podium when our name was called. When it was my turn, President Clinton introduced me with these words:

> In 1976, the Girl Scouts of America, one of our country's greatest institutions, was near collapse. Frances Hesselbein, a former volunteer from Johnstown, Pennsylvania, led them back, both in numbers and in spirit. She achieved not only the greatest diversity in the group's long history, but also its greatest cohesion, and in so doing, made a model for us all.
>
> In her current role as the President of the Peter Drucker Foundation for Nonprofit Management, she has shared her remarkable recipe for inclusion and excellence with countless organizations whose bottom line is measured not in dollars, but in changed lives.

Since Mrs. Hesselbein forbids the use of hierarchical words like "up" and "down" when she's around, I will call this pioneer for women, volunteerism, diversity and opportunity not up, but forward, to be recognized.

As I walked toward the president, I thought of my family and all the experiences I had had in the mountains of western Pennsylvania that helped shape my life, that determined the person I would be and the leader I would become.

My leadership journey started a long time before that moment at the White House, in the small town of Johnstown in the Allegheny Mountains of western Pennsylvania, known for the famous Johnstown flood of 1889. In my early teens, in the formative years before I would play all kinds of leadership roles in national and international organizations, I never thought of myself as a leader. I was never a class president, student government officer, or the editor of the school paper—never the leader. I had a different focus. I was very sure I would be writing poetry for the rest of my life. I had books everywhere; a quiet studious life lay ahead for me. Leading and managing were the furthest things from my mind.

But as I look back, everything I learned in Johnstown prepared me for my life in leadership. The rich diversity of the Johnstown schools prepared a child like me to grow up, go anywhere in the world, and feel that that was where I belonged at that moment.

My leadership journey began long ago with a decision I made when I was seventeen years old.

The Beginning of My Journey

I was a freshman at the University of Pittsburgh's Junior College, which had recently been established on two floors of a beautiful Johnstown High School building—one of the earliest community colleges in the country. I was hungry for the learning my young professors would provide in an innovative junior college. Writing poetry had been my junior high school dream; in high school my focus shifted to writing for the theatre. At the junior college I developed my passion for writing. My mind was opening to all sorts of new adventures. My body, too. Something at Pitt unleashed an interest in sports. At five-foot-two, I even became a member of the women's basketball team, all of whom were six to ten inches taller than I was. (They were hard up that year.)

"Junior Pitt" was the perfect preface to the lifetime of learning I would pursue. I loved every minute. And then it came to an abrupt end.

Six weeks after the beginning of college, my father died from the results of malaria and intermittent fever he suffered while serving with the U.S. Army in Panama and the Philippines. When he was stricken with heart and lung failure, he tried to get support for his terrible illness from the Veterans Administration, but they rejected his plea, declaring his condition "Not Service Related."

Despite this rejection, he loved his Army and his country to his last breath. As he lay dying in the hospital, he looked

at me and said, "I wish they could see the old soldier, now."
I was stroking his cheek. (My mother was out in the hall,
unable to face the ending.) As I kissed his forehead in those
last minutes, I said, "Daddy, don't worry about Mother and
the kids. I'll take care of the family." A tear rolled down my
father's cheek. I kissed it and he was gone.

We buried my father on a sunny October day and
came back from the cemetery to my grandfather's house. We
were sitting in the same beautiful music room where my
father's body had been lying during the funeral service only
a few hours ago. We sat in a small circle, my mother, sister,
brother, Mama Wicks and Papa Wicks (our grandparents),
Aunt Carrie and Uncle Mike, and Aunt Frances and Uncle
Walter from Philadelphia. There had been many embraces
and tears, of course, and then the conversation. Aunt Frances,
in her most gentle, loving way said, "Frances, we want you to
come to Philadelphia when this semester is over, live with us,
and attend Swarthmore College. Your uncle and I will take
care of everything, your tuition, books, whatever you need.
We want you to finish college." Philadelphia was a long way
across the state from my hometown.

Then my grandfather, Papa Wicks, said, "Sadie and I
want your mother and Trudy and John to come to live with
us while you are in school. We have this big house, five
bedrooms, and no one here but Mama and me. It would be
the greatest joy for us to have your mother and brother and
sister live with us while you finish college." I looked at my
mother, who had lived in that house when she was one of
seven children. Grief stricken, my mother remained silent.
The conversation was directed at me. At seventeen, I was

4

asked to make a decision that would affect our lives forever, as I realized later.

I looked at the sun shining through the stained-glass windows I had loved as a child, and tried to imagine life without my father, what would happen without him. I thought of my promise to him as he lay dying. I said, "I think my father would want us to stay together. I'll finish this semester, and in January find a job and take college classes at night." And I went on to describe the future with such feeling that my whole family supported me. There were tears. My Philadelphia aunt and uncle were disappointed but loving in their acceptance of my decision, as were my grandparents. No one argued. They loved and respected this seventeen-year-old who was called to keep a small family together.

We were driven back to Johnstown, and my mother; sister, Trudy, thirteen; brother, John, eleven; and I began life without the father we loved so dearly. I continued my Pitt classes eager for each day, aware that this was my last full-time semester.

Two young professors and their wives were wonderfully supportive. The professors, Dr. Doren Tharp (English) and Dr. Nathan Shappee (History), watched over me, even arranged for me to "audit" some graduate evening courses. Taking a few classes, auditing others, and reading and writing—the adventure in learning was measured not by credits but by substance. This was a rich, generous learning experience that would serve me well on the path ahead. Even after earning many credits and taking ever more classes, I never did get a formal degree, but I had begun a lifelong journey of learning that continues to be a joy to this day.

When the semester ended, I went to apply for a job wearing my best suit, high heels, and my mother's pretty wide-brimmed hat, with my long pageboy hair in a bun. I was interviewed by Mr. Corbin, the vice president of marketing and advertising at the Penn Traffic Company (a great department store, and part of the city's cultural center), who didn't realize I was only eighteen. (He didn't ask my age.) I worked as his assistant in advertising and marketing and then as the decorating consultant helping people design their interiors in the store's new model home. One day, Mr. Corbin asked me about some flowers on my desk, and I replied that it was my nineteenth birthday. He was shocked and said, "You're nothing but a god damn baby." But he kept me on. I stayed until I married John Hesselbein three years later.

Learn by Doing

Don't ask what training I had to prepare me for the work I did. Much of my learning in those early years and later took place while doing. I did what I needed to do, what I was called to do, and had a successful early career until I married John Hesselbein, and another great adventure began.

As a young adult and mother of an eight-year-old son, I received my early management training as a Girl Scout troop leader. Later I became the chairman of the United Way in Johnstown. These experiences taught me lessons in mobilizing diverse people and groups together around mission and vision to achieve a common goal, and demonstrated the power of finding common ground. Living in a community that had not always appreciated its rich diversity, I knew I had to be courageous and fight for inclusion, equal opportunity, and equal access for all. I could not have learned any of this in a classroom.

In 1976, in New York City, I was offered the position of National Executive Director (CEO) of the Girl Scouts of the USA. I loved every one of my five thousand days, thirteen years as the executive director of the largest organization for girls and women in the world.

To this day, I carry with me the lessons I've learned on this long journey, whether I learned them at my grandmother's knee, in a dialogue with students on a college campus, with a roomful of executives from great corporations, or in a country far across the world. In June 2009, I spoke to Drucker Society gatherings in Korea, the sixty-eighth country in which I have spoken or represented my country. Every global encounter is a rich learning experience, one that is much more than an exposure to the culture, the arts, the history, or the current political situation. Such experiences are about the hearts and minds and friendships that make us who we are and bind us together in the human family.

∞

It was a long way from my grandfather's music room to that day in the White House with President Clinton, yet a lifetime of learning took place from the day when the funeral was over, and a young girl began a journey—an adventure in learning that would accompany me wherever I would go.

When I made my decision to keep the family together, not to go to Swarthmore, it was all about purpose, as I would recognize later. My purpose was to keep my family together, as my father would have wanted me to do.

I did not aspire to be a leader, or seek out opportunities to lead. Doors opened. When I look at my journey—the many doors that were opened for me and the doors I opened myself—I have to ask, Who am I that people open doors for me? How have I been able to open doors for others? It is hard to distill the qualities needed in response to Emerson's "Be ye an opener of doors." In who I am, I work hard to live by my values every day: respect, love, inclusion, listening, and sharing.

Perhaps in this chronicle I can explain why sharing my adventure in leadership begins with the person I have become, with who I am, and why the journey continues on. I have many questions to explore: What are the lessons learned? Rarely do we travel alone, so who are our fellow travelers? Did we choose them, or did they just appear? When do we say welcome; when do we say good-bye? Are there a few principles that guide us? What are the stops along the way? And when do we make the great discovery that *leadership is a journey, not a destination?*

PART ONE

ROOTS

CHAPTER 1

STORIES OF FAMILY, LESSONS OF LOVE

Whenever I hear that someone is a "self-made" man or woman, I smile. None of us is truly self-made. We all stand on the shoulders of those who have gone before us, and we all have reason to be grateful for the help we have received along the way.

In my own life, I have many reasons to be grateful. I remember a Girl Scout message from an earlier day, "Honor the past. Cherish the future." Both are equally important. If we do not honor the past, we may well end up thinking everything begins and ends with us. Such self-centeredness leads to swollen egos—and pride, which, as we all know, goeth before the fall.

Lessons of Love and Family

In my lifetime, with all the remarkable guides, family, and friends who made it all possible, there is one person who has had the greatest influence on my life and my work—my grandmother Sadie Pringle Wicks. This surprises people, for some of the greatest thought leaders in many fields have shared my journey in generous and highly visible ways. Yet from the time I could walk and talk and say, "Mama Wicks," she had the greatest impact on me—personally, with my family, and professionally. She was small, gentle, loving, and quiet. She was always there for me. Her wisdom, her depth, and her love began to shape me from my earliest years. When I would walk in the room, I was the only person there. When she talked to me, I still remember, she would look into my eyes intently. For that moment she made me feel like the most important person in the world.

When I was a small child, she used to tell me family stories about our ancestors. For example, when Lincoln called for volunteers, the seven Pringle brothers, one of whom was Mama Wicks's father and my great-grandfather, set out with their father on the Pennsylvania Railroad train from Summerhill to Johnstown, nine miles away. First, the father walked with them to a photography studio, where he had each son photographed. Then they walked over to the post office, where they volunteered, and then the seven sons left for Pittsburgh to be inducted. The youngest was nineteen, the eldest twenty-seven. Six of these men were married, and left their wives and children and farms because their country called. It never occurred to them that three could go and four could stay at home and take care of their farms and their small lumber mill that made barrel staves way back in the mountains. All seven brothers volunteered. They were called to do what they did. At the end of the war, six brothers came home. The nineteen-year-old, the baby of the family, was fatally injured in the Battle of the Wilderness. One solider brother was given leave to bring Martin's body home. As a little girl, I would go with Mama Wicks to the Pringle Hill cemetery, our family burial ground, and we would pause at each weathered marble headstone as she told me stories about the seven Pringle brothers. With these visits and the stories, my grandmother showed me how to honor the past and the leaders in my family.

I experienced another example of my grandmother's influence not long after I was married and World War II began. My husband John volunteered for the Navy and was sent to Pensacola for training as a Naval Combat Air Crew photographer. It seemed a strange assignment for a young newspaper editor and writer, but off he went, saying good-bye to our eighteen-month-old Johnny and me.

I was determined to join him with the baby in Pensacola, but my mother, other family, and friends were horrified. Mother even suggested my leaving the baby with her and going alone. They had an extensive list of objections and excuses. It was a long train ride to Pensacola, he could be sent out as we arrived, and on and on. When in doubt, my practice was to ask Mama Wicks. She was the mother of nine children, with seven surviving, and had lived a long life with an adoring husband (so adoring that he wrote a long, passionate poem to her on their fiftieth wedding anniversary).

She listened to my story, put her arms around me, and said quietly, "Your place is with your husband and with the baby." I went back home and said, "Mama Wicks says my place is with my husband." No one could contradict Mama Wicks.

13

So, by Pennsylvania Railroad, from Johnstown, Pennsylvania, to Pensacola, Florida, with my eighteen-month-old baby, John, and his crib so he would feel at home, I traveled to be with big John. Later, after this trip, we took an even longer train ride from Pensacola to San Diego Naval Air Base to be with John. Those few years in naval towns, with very little money, were some of the best years of our lives. I took little Johnny to the beach while his father was flying; I'd say prayers and sometimes smile while thinking that a guy who had never even shot a BB gun was in a clear bubble under the plane with a camera and a big gun. John was told, "You shoot your way in, and shoot pictures on the way out. And as you are leaning out to shoot pictures, if you drop the camera, just follow it." Navy training humor.

The war ended as John was finally to be deployed. Johnny and I came home to Johnstown by train in time for Christmas. The eighteen-month-old baby was now four years old. John didn't get discharged until February, and came home to find the Christmas tree still up, losing needles, yet with lights, ornaments, and gifts under the tree to welcome our sailor home.

Mama Wicks died before our tour of duty was over. Her simple statement, "Your place is with your husband," taught me lessons about the power of love and about families belonging together. What a different life it would have been if I had heeded the timid ones who told me it was too dangerous to take the baby thousands of miles by train. Later, when I was called to give advice in many difficult situations, I learned to consider the issue and simply state from the heart my best advice, and it is always about them, not you. My grandmother taught me this.

The second-greatest influence on my life was Mama Wicks's daughter Carrie—my beloved Aunt Carrie who had a greater influence on my work and who I am today than my own mother.

Here in its entirety is the letter she sent to me on my birthday in 1985, which shows that the admiration was mutual.

Easton, PA

Dearest Frances:

The enclosed photograph of you, Mom and Pop will tell you how long you and I have been "Travel Companions". [The photograph was of my grandparents with me as a six- or seven-year-old.] This was the last time you came with anyone. From that time on you came alone, or, with me when I had been visiting in South Fork.

I have such happy memories of those days. When you were four or five years old, I asked your opinions of so many things, such as, which dress I should wear to a party etc., and that has gone on through the years; of course you came to me for counsel. Well all in all, we have been good "Buddies." Do you remember the time you came to Easton from New York in a blizzard after you had attended a National Board Meeting? You had to come in a bus via Reading, Pa.

You always went the second mile for Mike and me.

I knew, from the time you were five years old (in kindergarten) that you were destined to do great things and that Prophecy has come true. I do love you and hope all your wishes will be granted.

> *"He who would do wonderful things very often must travel alone."*
>
> Henry Van Dyke

A happy, happy Birthday and dearest love to you.

Carrie

October 28, 1985

My husband appreciated Aunt Carrie almost as much as I did, and we loved including her in our travels. We smiled together during a trip to Paris when, in her late eighties, she sprinted up the long stairs to the top of the Basilica of the Sacre-Coeur, even though an electric lift was available. While in the United Kingdom, we also noticed that no one was more absorbed, more appreciative of the King's Library in the British Museum than Carrie.

Carrie's father was born in Tywardreath, a tiny village in Cornwall, England, a village of farmers, fishermen, and tin miners, who heard long ago the message of John Wesley and built a little Methodist chapel outside the village walls in the late 1700s. The great landowners would not permit "the dissidents" to build the chapel within the village walls at that time.

However, by 1823, this sturdy little band had grown so strong and so determined that they persuaded a farmer in the village to let them build their Methodist chapel on his land within the village walls. He agreed on one condition: on one side of the church wall, there had to be a lean-to for his cows. So for years, there were no windows on one side of the church.

Church history records that in 1823, three farmers were ordained as lay preachers, and every Sunday after service, these sturdy lay preachers who were farmers and tin miners walked to nearby villages to preach the Word. Our ancestor, Thomas Henry Wicks, was one of those three. So Carrie and I would go to Cornwall every year; sit in the 1823 Wicks pew; and think about our courageous, "dissident" ancestors; and I would hope that their genes, their blood still flowed in my generation, and I would say to myself, "I'm the sixth generation of dissidents to sit in this pew, and I'm not going to change." You can find great strength in honoring the past even as you cherish the future. Carrie helped teach me this.

Carrie was regent of a Daughters of the American Revolution chapter and helped save and restore historic eighteenth-century buildings in Easton, Pennsylvania, where I now have a home. I think she added to my love of history, of family heritage, and of the men and women who sustained the democracy in every war from the French and Indian War and the Revolutionary War to the War of 1812, and to my appreciation for the seven Pringle brothers who fought in the Civil War. All the men in our family served in World War II. My father and my son served in the U.S. Army and loved it. My son is now on oxygen twenty-four hours a day, has a faltering heart, and is confined to his bed, but says proudly, "I was a soldier, I am a soldier, I will always be a soldier." He writes his own books and feels as I do about family and country. When I call every evening and ask how he is, "Mom, I'm doing great" is his answer, and we talk about his writing and his new granddaughter, Isabella Frances Hesselbein, the joy of his life. Service is a value that runs strong in my family.

My son and Carrie were very close from the time he was a baby. She bought him his first cowboy boots when he was six, and I often hear her voice when he is talking with me about the U.S. Army, for she was a great Army historian.

Carrie died at ninety-six, still the bright, charming, impeccably groomed, tastefully dressed, perfect companion I will always remember. At every wonderful event in my career she was there, in New York, in Washington, wherever, adding a special and loving dimension to the moment. I carry her in my heart always.

My Father

Long ago, my father, who was traveling, wrote a letter with three sections: a short story about a bunny and a robin for my brother, John, who was two years old; a long poem filled with birds, animals, and children for my sister, Trudy, who was four years old; and a loving message to me, his eight-year-old: "Be good, be kind, be considerate of the feelings of others, and know your daddy loves you dearly."

At eight, I probably wanted some robins and bunnies of my own, yet as I was the one who read my father's loving messages to Trudy and John, over and over, I guess they became mine as well, and I tried to be what he wanted me to be. It's possible that so long ago, I learned that we take care of others. Later, this surely became part of my leadership approach, my commitment, and my belief that to serve is to live.

My father, Burgess Harmon Richards, was my hero for many reasons. He spent many years in the Army, serving on many fronts, from the Philippines and Panama to here in the United States, and he loved his Army years. On my wall are photographs of this sturdy, handsome guy in his football uniform as a fullback on the Willoughby, Ohio, high school championship football team, and on the U.S. Army and Pennsylvania State Police football teams.

He left the Army to become one of the first state police officers in Pennsylvania, which had established the first state police force in the country because of the violence in its coal towns, where ethnic groups were battling with one another. (Miners came from all over the world to work in the Pennsylvania coal mines.) General Norman Schwarzkopf's father was the man charged with forming this first state police force, at the request of the president of the United States. The call went out, and two thousand men applied, many of them U.S. Army cavalrymen. Two hundred were chosen, and my father was one of them. According to State of Pennsylvania archives, he was "an officer of great character and courage." These mounted policemen wore black uniforms and tall black caps, and rode big, dark horses. The miners from Eastern Europe dubbed them "the Black Hussars," for they reminded them of the czar's Hussars, who wore similar uniforms. (There is a book, *The Black Hussars*, that records the story of this historic force.) I have photographs of my father mounted on "Old High," his wonderful horse, in a parade. The battling miners were not afraid of guns, but when two Pennsylvania State Policemen galloped into the fray on those big animals, they disbursed.

My father was a great storyteller. His stories live with me today and still guide me. Best of all, he made our family history come alive. One story was especially poignant: in 1803, William Richards and Mary Adams were traveling in an oxcart from Connecticut to the Western Reserve of Connecticut (later to become Ohio), when their little girl was bitten by a rattlesnake and died. These early settlers endured hardships and made sacrifices that would inspire later generations of our family.

My father also told me about the certificate, now framed and hanging on my wall in Easton, that says, "William Richards, 1853, $150 contribution to the Western Reserve Eclectic Institute" (later to become Hiram College). He was one of the founders and then a trustee of the Institute. I think about this giving man, William Richards, a farmer, dedicated to education. In 1853, $150 was a huge amount of money. "How much better is wisdom than gold" he would inscribe in his books.

Generations later, my father's father, the Reverend Orphanus Quincy Adams Richards, graduated from Hiram College, Ohio, at nineteen, and married Serena Harmon (a freshman, fifteen), later the valedictorian of her class at Willoughby College (now Lake Erie College). When my grandfather was ordained a minister in the Disciples of Christ Church, the young couple was called to go to frontier towns in Wisconsin, to build Christian churches and congregations. Once a church was established in one town, they would go on to another. His sermons, which we treasure, are soaring, masterful, and poignant.

I never knew the Reverend Orphanus Quincy Adams Richards, but he remains alive for me because of my father's stories. He told me that when his father, the minister, heard that the miners in the Klondike gold rush were not hearing the Word of God, he took a leave of absence from his Pennsylvania church, bought big boots and "heavy gold rush clothing," took his eldest son, and went off to the Klondike to preach in tents and in ice fields, wherever the gold miners were. He observed that world.

When he came back, his lectures on Alaska were famous. A flyer for a January 24, 1899, lecture in Cleveland is head-lined, "Lecture by Rev. O. A. Richards of Beaver Falls, Pennsylvania, A Gold-Seeker's Experiences in Alaska." The flyer provides the subjects to be covered: "The Copper River Indians, Ocean voyage, sledding Trip into the Interior, Scaling an Ice Mountain 5,000 feet high, Boat-building, Shooting the Klutena Rapids, Prospecting for Gold with a Pack Train Through the Wilderness. Admission, 25 cents; Children, 15 cents. Family Tickets, $1.00." What an adventure!

My father was a fine writer. He wrote stories and even a book, which was lost along the way. He helped us appreciate the power of language as well as history. One day, when I was in grade school, I began calling him "Father," probably because I read a book in which the title impressed me. When I continued the "Father," one day he hugged me and said, "I think 'Daddy' will do." I got the loving message. "Daddy" it was.

A powerful sense of history, of family, and of service and obligation were all part of what Orphanus and Burgess left to their children, grandchildren, and now a new generation eager for the stories of their lives and the lessons they teach. And now it is time for my story—the stories of my life I am endeavoring to share.

It was wonderful that both my father and my mother's mother, Mama Wicks, were such impassioned storytellers and that they spent endless hours telling stories to a little girl who would ask for more, for stories to be repeated so that she could then tell them to her little boy, John, years later.

My Aunt Frances, my father's sister, told me stories particularly about our Adams ancestors. She had John Adams's own toddy bowl on her breakfront in her dining room in Philadelphia. I loved her stories about John and Abigail Adams. Only recently did I learn that John Adams was the only founding father who did not own a slave. That part of our family history comes alive once more as I read recent books on Adams and view the HBO series *John Adams* on DVD.

My niece Frances Chadwick Eckman, my sister's daughter and a great amateur genealogist, and I now keep alive the family stories my father passed along: Anyone for the French and Indian War? Or how about William Pringle, Private No. 19, Continental Militia, Pennsylvania? He came from Scotland to fight in our Revolutionary War. Or our great-great-grandmother's recipe for soap? And how does a young mother tell her husband on a Civil War battlefield that their eighteen-month-old little girl has died of diphtheria "and there are no men left to dig the grave. Two little boys eleven years old from nearby farms dug the grave and their mothers laid out her little body." Family Civil War letters keep alive the stories of the courage and the sacrifice of Mary and Philip Pringle and all the men and women who have gone before us—who lived and sacrificed so that we could live our lives as we do today.

These are the stories we heard as children from my beloved grandmother; father; Aunt Carrie; and Harry and Ida, John's parents, whose people lived through the Johnstown Flood of 1889—and these are the stories of their lives I share—lessons learned along the way to be applied in our lives.

Because of my father's age—he was forty when I was born—my grandfather could have been my great-grandfather, and although I missed knowing him as a person, his amazing, colorful life, the way he wrote, and this personal window on an earlier generation were great gifts passed down by my father and his stories. So we three children loved, absorbed, and lived lives shaped by the stories our father told us. I cherish those stories, and they are as vivid and alive as they were long ago. My love and respect for the military, the Army, police officers—all those who lay their lives on the line every day for all of us—began with my father, the time he took to tell his children the stories of his young life and all the ways he served his country. Stories of family and life told by a loved one have amazing impact.

With what my father taught us, my brother and sister and I stayed close as we grew up, got married, and ended up living in three parts of the world—John in California and Oregon, I in Pennsylvania and New York, and Trudy with her Navy husband, Captain Walter D. Chadwick, all over the world, wherever submarines dock. Somehow we stayed closer than most families, to this day. Trudy and John have left us, but are very much alive in my life and work.

Although I lost my father at seventeen, he stays with me. His example of writing and storytelling, his sense of history and our heritage, and his love of family and service walk around with me. I think of him every day and am grateful to a soldier, "an officer of great character and courage," who adored his children; understood the power of love, language, and example; and tried to prepare Trudy, John, and me for a life well lived, a life of service. Today, when I am working with cadets at West Point and with U.S. Army Chiefs of Staff, my father is smiling.

My Husband

I married into a Johnstown, Pennsylvania, newspaper family. Harry Hesselbein, my husband's father, was managing editor of the *Tribune* for many years and active in the community. Harry Hesselbein, "Bastion of integrity," is what he was called in an essay in the *Johnstown Tribune* on its 150th birthday. Harry and Ida Davis Hesselbein were the finest people I have ever known. Both were from early Johnstown families, both families surviving the 1889 flood. I was so fortunate to become their daughter, and I think of them every day.

When John graduated from the University of Pittsburgh as a journalism major, he went to work as the night city editor of the *Johnstown Democrat*. When we were first married, I thought that his was the most romantic career in the world.

After the war, we came back home to Johnstown, where John set up his own business—the Hesselbein Studios. There John made award-winning documentaries and was named a Robert Flaherty Fellow, one of the first six in the United States. (Robert Flaherty was the father of the American documentary.) John also initiated an early local television program, *Adventuring in the Arts*.

Our studio did all kinds of photography: high school senior portraits, belching steel mills at night, weddings—whatever the customer wanted, we tried to provide. John was the artist, and our young teenager, Johnny, assisted in the darkroom. I did something I called "helping John." In a small family-owned business, everyone helps. So I helped with the documentary films John made, with all kinds of photography—not the artistic shooting, but the preparation of the final product—marketing, listening to the customer, meeting their needs, and so on. I worked on *Adventuring in the Arts*. When a customer wanted her dog's photograph to look like a painting, John handed me some oil paints, and the customer soon had an oil painting of her dog. I loved my life with those two John Hesselbeins, never wanted to leave Johnstown and never expected to.

Little did I know that everything I learned by doing, by "helping John," would provide me with indispensable skills, tools, and a background I would need in the future I had never envisioned, one I never thought I wanted when it came. Communications was our business, and communications became a basis for my work years later. Providence plays an important part in the story of my life. There is a plan, was a plan, from the beginning. I just was unaware that everything I did was preparing me for the life I would live, the contribution I would try to make in the years ahead. I never wanted to leave Pennsylvania or my hometown. Little did I know that Providence was at work, or that a whole new world of opportunity, of service, and of fulfillment was waiting.

CHAPTER 2

EMBRACE THE
DEFINING MOMENT

Today, when we observe the lowest level of trust and the highest level of cynicism, the call for leaders who are healers and unifiers must be heard. Wherever we are, whatever our work, whatever our platform or forum, we must find the language that heals, the inclusion that unifies. It is a critical time for leaders at every level to make the difference, and demonstrate that respect for all people is a paramount value. "For if the trumpet gives an uncertain sound, who shall prepare himself to the battle?" should be a powerful reminder for all of us.

Sometimes when we hear that call, we can look back in our own family history and recognize a connection, a force that moved us toward the defining moments in our life that shaped the person we would be, the leader we would become. We find the moments in our life when someone helped shine a light that would illuminate our future and the lives of all whom we will touch. For me, there were a few such critical moments.

Take Care of Others

I am four years older than my sister, Trudy, and have loved her dearly all her life. When I was eight years old and she was four, my mother would say, over and over in all kinds of situations, "Take care of your little sister." And I did.

I remember the Christmas when I had just turned eight (my birthday is November 1), and my father had built two beautiful baby doll beds of wood and painted them ivory. Our Aunt Gertrude knitted pink wool baby bonnets and sweaters, and my grandmother made baby quilts for the two little beds. To fill the beds, our parents found two darling baby dolls that looked just like new babies, with big eyes that opened when you held them up and closed when you laid them down in their little beds.

I've never had a Christmas present I loved more. That Christmas morning was a joy I still remember.

A few days later, I came home from playing in the snow, went over to see my baby doll under the Christmas tree, and found that her little bed was empty. Trudy's doll was soundly asleep in hers.

I ran to my mother saying, "My baby doll is gone," and she said, "Annie's little girl did not get a doll for Christmas, so I gave her your doll." (Annie was our cleaning lady.)

I cried and cried, and my mother said, "You're too old for dolls anyway."

That was my last doll, although I kept the bed and my grandmother's baby quilt for a long time. I guess I grew up in a special way that Christmas. I don't know why I remember that one moment in my childhood, the loss of my baby doll; maybe it was because at eight I learned that I had no right to that baby doll, that I was too old. I guess I also learned on that day long ago that we take care of others. This lesson stayed with me on my journey to leadership and helped foster my commitment to the idea that to serve is to live.

I often wonder how many of us who work in the social sector, contribute as volunteers, or provide financial support to meet critical needs somehow learned early on, as children, that we help other people. Many of us learn that we are responsible for others, responsible for family, friends, the whole community, society, and, in the end, the democracy. This somehow begins when we are children—taking care of our little sisters and brothers or others in our community who are in need.

As hard as it was to lose my baby doll or to miss playtime with friends because I was taking care of my sister, these are the same lessons learned by the millions of us who try to take care of others, to open doors, and to change lives, especially our own.

Respect for All

Not too long ago, I was speaking to a large group of corporate chief learning officers, and after my speech we had a very open and engaging dialogue. The last question asked was, "Mrs. Hesselbein, what was the one defining moment that determined the person you would be—the leader you would become?" No one had ever asked me this before, yet I knew the answer immediately and responded.

When I was eight years old, I told the executives, I was visiting my grandparents in South Fork, Pennsylvania, a small coal-mining and railroad town nine miles from my home in Johnstown. My grandfather Papa Wicks had a men's clothing store, was Justice of the Peace, and played the pipe organ in the Methodist Church every Sunday.

I adored my grandparents and spent every weekend with Mama and Papa Wicks. They had seven children, so they needed a big house, and it seemed only logical to them to build a music room with a sixteen-foot ceiling and a pipe organ. With stained-glass windows that caught the sunlight, the music room was my favorite place. On the shelf above the pipe organ keyboard were two beautiful old Chinese vases. I would try to coax my grandmother into letting me play with them, and she always said no. Finally, on one Saturday visit, I became very assertive. I actually stamped my foot at my grandmother and demanded that I be allowed to play with the vases. Instead of scolding me, she led me over to a small love seat facing the pipe organ, put her arms around me, and told me this story:

> Long ago, when your mother was about your age, some days she and her little sisters would come home from school crying that some bad boys were chasing Mr. Yee and calling him bad names. Now, in this little town was a Chinese laundryman, who lived alone in his small laundry. Each week he picked up your grandfather's shirts and brought them back in a few days, washed, starched, and ironed perfectly. Mr. Yee wore traditional Chinese dress—a long tunic and a cap with his hair in a queue. The boys would chase

30

him, yelling, "Chinky, Chinky Chinaman," and worse.
They would try to pull his queue.

One day there was a knock on the kitchen door.
When I opened it, there stood Mr. Yee, with a large
package in his arms. I said, "Oh, Mr. Yee, please come
in. Won't you sit down?" But Mr. Yee just stood there
and handed me the package, saying, "This is for you."
I opened the package, and in it were two beautiful old
Chinese vases. I said, "Mr. Yee, these are too valuable.
I couldn't accept them." His answer was, "I want you
to have them." I asked, "Why do you want me to have
them?"

He said, "Mrs. Wicks, I have been in this town for
ten years, and you are the only one who ever called me
Mr. Yee. They won't let me bring my wife and children
here, and I miss them too much, so I am going back to
China. The vases are all I brought with me. I want you
to have them." There were tears in his eyes as he said
good-bye.

In my grandmother's arms, I cried my heart out for poor
Mr. Yee. That was long ago, but nevertheless the defining
moment when I learned that all people deserve respect,
a moment that would stay with me, shaping my life with a
passion for diversity and inclusion. My grandmother wanted
me to have those vases when she died, and today they sit on a
shelf in my living room at my home in Easton. Do you think
I ever walk into that room, see the vases on a shelf, and not
think of Mr. Yee and Mama Wicks?

Years later, as I have already recounted, I was at the
White House to receive our country's highest civilian award,

31

the Presidential Medal of Freedom. My grandmother and Mr. Yee were with me.

Fighting Discrimination

My husband John loved jazz, and his favorite artist was Duke Ellington, who used to bring his orchestra to play in a theater in our hometown. We had all his records and went to every one of his concerts in Johnstown, and sometimes those in New York. Duke Ellington and his band were the royalty of jazz. Still are.

The duke's history was long in our town. Part of it was sad, for in the early days, he and his band members were not allowed to stay in a hotel in town; they stayed with other black families instead. Then the day came when they could stay at the Fort Stanwix Hotel, but when they ate in the dining room, screens blocked them off from the other diners. Finally, the time came when the great Duke Ellington and his band could stay and dine at the hotel with no restrictions.

When I learned this story, probably in my early twenties, it broke my heart that this inimitable artist, musician, and American, honored both here and abroad, suffered the indignities of discrimination early in his career in my beloved hometown.

By the time I was growing up, the community had changed, and I could write about my experience in an exuberant way, yet I never forgot that at one time Duke Ellington could not sleep in a hotel or eat in a hotel dining room in my hometown.

In those days, there were many kinds of discrimination against black people even in this open, wonderfully diverse industrial community. One day, my husband received a call from the office of Pennsylvania's governor. He was asked to serve on a new Pennsylvania Human Relations Commission, along with a young Catholic priest in our town, Father Philip Saylor.

When there were reports to the commission of discrimination against a minority in Johnstown, John or Father Saylor would be informed, and it was their job to call on the offender and explain why the discriminatory behavior could not continue. They were equal rights ambassadors.

I remember several examples. One was a barbershop that was refusing to cut black people's hair. John's task was to call on the barber, telling him that all people must be served. "Their hair is different," the barber said, "and I don't have the right tools." My husband's reply: "Then you will have to buy the right tools."

Once, Father Saylor called on a steel company executive to share a complaint that all of the 300 foremen were white. Result: by the following Monday, Bethlehem Steel had its first black foreman.

Of course, there was also resistance. A white teacher, seeing a black woman and her two children on a school playground, yelled, "You niggers get off the playground." John called on her to calmly discuss the incident. "You are a traitor to your race," she responded.

This work was not something a young businessman or a young Catholic priest should have been doing, in the opinion of many. It took courage in those days to serve on a human rights commission in a small town in the mountains of western Pennsylvania. And it never occurred to me to say, "John, don't you think you should be a little less visible, or less public?" I always thought he was doing what he was meant to be doing, and of course his volunteer work became a natural part of everything I did. One day at the studio, when a customer's order was not ready, we were shocked by the woman's response: "If I were a member of the NAACP, I'm sure it would be ready." Our support for civil rights was not wonderful advertising for our business as far as some people were concerned, but we happened to think that sticking to our principles came first. I was proud of John's contribution in supporting equal rights and respect for all people, when it was not a popular position.

One time when an African American staff member on the Governor's Commission was in Johnstown, he and Father Saylor went in to the local downtown restaurant that was everyone's favorite. As they sat down at a table, the waiter said to Father Saylor, "We don't serve them here," pointing to the guest. "Tonight you do," said the young priest. From then on, "they" were served, and discrimination against minorities was ended in the restaurants of our town. All it took was the courage of one citizen to break a barrier that was already crumbling. I could feel my ancestors, Civil War veterans, resting more comfortably in their graves. Almost a hundred years after the Civil War, we were still fighting the battle they died for. And we still are today.

A Part of My Life and Work

Through hearing such stories of my grandmother and Mr. Yee, Duke Ellington, and of my husband and the Pennsylvania Human Relations Commission, I incorporated the values of respect for and inclusion of all people into my life, work, and message.

These values were reinforced by my early experiences with the Girl Scouts. Before the civil rights movement of the 1960s, I served as the director of the Blue Knob Girl Scout Camp in the Appalachian mountains. Photographs from the time showed our respect for diversity. In one, our gifted assistant camp director, Rose Hawkins, a great leader who was a black woman, is smiling beside me in a picture of our Girl Scout camp staff.

Rose Hawkins, who worked in a dress factory, is the wise leader who counseled me to "carry a big basket," which I will tell you about in Chapter Four. She is one of my heroes. She and I had small children in those early Girl Scout days, and I know my son's exposure to Rose Hawkins, when he was a "junior handy boy" at our Girl Scout camp later, enriched his life and the leader he would become, as it did mine.

In 1976, when I was being considered for the position of executive director of the Girl Scouts of the USA, I was asked to provide a letter of reference from a female Johnstown leader; most of the key references were from distinguished male leaders. So I asked Mabel Johnson, a great community leader, local Girl Scout board member, and wonderful friend, to write to the search committee. I did not mention that she was black. She was the wife of my husband's dentist and knew me very well. Mabel, as I remember, was chairman of the NAACP membership drive, and we signed on as members every year. Two years later, after John's death in 1978, several Girl Scout national board members were at the funeral home viewing in Johnstown, and I introduced them to Mabel and

Dr. Johnson. One board member later remarked to me, "You didn't tell us Mrs. Johnson was black." Her being black would have been a positive addition in their eyes, but her race had nothing to do with why I asked her for a reference.

What were some of the lessons learned in that big steel, big coal, big labor, big hearts town that I carry with me?

The power of inclusion.

The power of diversity.

"The first woman who" has less to do with gender, more to do with performance.

The power of the essential principle called "courage to lead."

The power of language: "When they look at us, can they find themselves?"

The power of mission, of values, of innovation, of diversity and inclusion—and all have to be part of every aspect of the enterprise.

Preaching Won't Do the Job

The defining moments in my own life and work meant that diversity and inclusion would be vital ingredients of whatever I was called to do. A defining moment is something that really changes you inside—it goes far beyond lip service. We can preach mission and values, put them on a plaque on the wall, and print them in the annual report, yet unless we live them every day of our lives, we fail. The people we work with watch us closely, and when we embody our mission and values in all we say, all we do, and how we lead, the result is a highly motivated, highly productive workforce. We light their fire.

However, if we speak one way yet lead, behave, and act in the opposite way, the result is a dispirited, unmotivated, and unproductive workforce. No fire, just getting by.

If we value diversity and inclusion, then we must ask, "When they look at us, can they find themselves?" This is the powerful question that uncovers whether an organization practices what it preaches. If the response is a resounding "Yes," then indeed the organization is a viable, relevant organization of the future. We asked ourselves that question at the Girl Scouts of the USA, and the result was that in a few years we more than tripled racial and ethnic representation across the organization, at every level.

In my early years at the national organization, as we were working hard to make sure people of all races and backgrounds could find themselves in our organization, I met a business leader who took me aside and said, "Frances, I really care about you and the organization, but you have to stop this diversity stuff. Nobody wants to hear about it, and if you keep it up you will never raise any money!" I thanked him politely and went out and recruited John Creedon, who was the new president of MetLife; and with his three wonderful cochairs, we raised $10 million for our new Edith Macy Conference Center on four hundred beautiful wooded acres in Westchester County that we owned. It was symbolic of where the organization was headed.

Today, wherever I serve, wherever I go, my fellow travelers and colleagues always represent the face of America. We are fellow travelers not because of race and ethnicity, but diversity does add a special dimension to the experience of the leaders who share the journey. It is not an accident that of the six photographs of U.S. Army generals on my office wall, four are African American—great generals I have worked with and spoken for recently. The U.S. Army is the face of America.

To this day, I go where I am called to go, and I carry with me lessons learned long ago, learned last month, and learned last week. Nowhere do I encounter a hunger for "the good old days." The leaders in all three sectors with whom I spend my time are ready to lead into the future, building organizations of the future, even though none of us can yet describe that future. As great as the ambiguities are, there are remarkable leaders in all three sectors who are taking the lead with a call to action that will mobilize us all. In the end, it will not be one big message or one big voice, but millions of us, in our own way, healing, unifying, and experiencing that defining moment when we recognize that respect for all people is essential to sustaining the democracy.

CHAPTER 3

DEFINING YOURSELF WITH THE POWER OF NO

The great Peter Drucker admonished us to "Focus, focus, focus." (He never said it once.) "Focus, focus, focus" drives us to pay attention to those few things, those critical initiatives that determine relevance, viability, and success in the future—and this reverberating phrase walks around with many of us who worked with Peter. We can focus only if we learn to say no to opportunities that aren't right for us, individually or organizationally. In this way, we continuously define ourselves as well as our purpose in life.

The Power of No

I first discovered the Power of No early, long before I met Peter Drucker. When I was six years old, in first grade, I brought my first report card home. My father looked at it with pleasure until he noticed the name and said, "There is some mistake. Your name is not Frances Ann Richards. It is Frances Willard Richards."

I replied, "Willard is a boy's name, and Frances Willard sounds like a boy; so I changed my name. I told my teacher, 'My name is Frances Ann Richards.'" (My mother's name was Ann.)

I waited for the scolding that never came. My father turned away, and I could see a small smile on his face.

Later, when I was older, he told me about his father's good friend Frances Elizabeth Willard, the founder of the Women's Christian Temperance Union (WCTU). Grandfather Richards shared her passion for "temperance." They were such close friends that when my grandfather's daughter (my aunt) was born, she was named Frances Willard Richards in honor of the founder of the WCTU. So, a generation later, when my father had me, his first baby girl, of course family tradition decreed that I would also be named Frances Willard Richards. But six years later, as my father discovered, I went to my teacher (Miss Alice Jones—the best teacher in the world to me) and asked her to change my name in her records, saying, "My name is Frances Ann." Miss Jones did what I asked.

This may seem a trivial incident, and it probably was, but I think it illustrates in a small way an approach to life that has served me well. We all need to define ourselves. No one else can define who we are, why we do what we do. If the name doesn't fit, we change it. If we are on the wrong bus in life, we get off; it is ours to do. Wrong seat, we change seats; wrong direction, we change vectors. If the name Willard doesn't communicate who we are, good-bye Willard, whether we are six or sixty.

The White House Is Calling

As an adult, I also appreciated the Power of No in understanding my calling—most memorably when I was invited to
the White House to discuss a possible cabinet position in the
Reagan administration. I first met President Reagan when
the Girl Scouts of the USA was about to have its seventieth
birthday in 1982. The president sent a message to my office
at the Girl Scout headquarters in New York, saying he would
like to host a luncheon at the White House to celebrate the
Girl Scout birthday, and would I please send him 125 names
of guests to invite to the luncheon. With great anticipation we
sent him the names, including young Girl Scouts, national
and Girl Scout council board and staff members, and a few
major supporters.

March 12 was Girl Scout Day at the White House, with
President and Mrs. Reagan hosting. I sat between President
Reagan and John Creedon (the president of MetLife, who, as
I mentioned in Chapter Two, had chaired our campaign to
raise $10 million to build the Edith Macy Conference Cen-
ter). During the luncheon, President Reagan spoke, paying a
moving tribute to that long green line of Girl Scouts going
back to 1912. When he sat down, he handed me his notes.

Later, in 1986, when we were bringing out our big Say
No to Drugs program, we asked Mrs. Reagan if she would
be our guest at a dinner in Washington at the Ritz-Carlton
to launch the program. Mrs. Reagan replied, "I never go out
at night without Ronnie, but I could make it to lunch." So
we had an elegant and enthusiastic luncheon with Nancy
Reagan, as she accepted the first Say No to Drugs Girl Scout

badge, beautifully framed. It was a high moment for Girl Scouts everywhere.

Sometime later, I received a call from the president's staff member responsible for Cabinet affairs. He invited me to come to Washington at President Reagan's request to discuss a potential appointment to a Cabinet-level position. What a tremendous honor—perhaps the greatest honor of my life. Yet I wasn't sure that this was the right move for me. I prayed all the way to Washington, wanting to make the right decision, for I knew it would be one of the most significant I would ever make.

It was very difficult then, as it is even more so today, for girls growing up. The Girl Scouts had developed a highly contemporary program and were in the middle of a remarkably new and expansive leadership development initiative with learning opportunities for everyone—all the volunteers, the board, and staff—and I knew we were making a difference. We were in the middle of this tremendously powerful transformation, and I was being called to Washington. I thought to myself, *Is this what I am called to do?*

When I arrived at the White House, I was ushered into a beautiful sitting room by President Reagan's representative. We sat down, and after his welcome, I said, "I've been thinking very hard ever since you called. It is a tremendous honor to be asked to serve my country, with this president, this White House. And yet I've concluded that the best way to serve my country is to continue serving as the CEO of the Girl Scouts of the USA. I believe right now that in our country, young people, young girls, Girl Scouts, need all the support we can give them. Please thank President Reagan for thinking of me. I am tremendously grateful, but I think I am called to continue to serve my country with the Girl Scouts." He was gracious and appreciative as we said good-bye.

I felt that if I left the Girl Scouts at that point, I would have abandoned the Movement. It would have been very difficult to maintain and sustain the momentum of the transformation if the organization were to be distracted by an executive search and the transition to a new leader. This was an amazing moment in the history of the Girl Scout Movement, and I was a part of it. I could not just step away from it at that point, no matter how honored I was to be asked to serve our country in the government, in a different role.

In the end, after I had thought about it, I was surprised at how clear my decision was. I had to stay with the Girl Scouts; it was where I belonged. I didn't agonize about it. I had no second thoughts, no regrets. Generations of my family had served our country in some way, and accepting this position would have probably been the ultimate, but serving girls was the call I had to respond to. Later, thinking back on it, I thought the moment had far less to do with me as an individual and far more to do with the Girl Scouts and those remarkable 650,000 volunteers and staff members, soon to be 766,000 in the service of our 2.25 million girls and young women.

My decision to say no was clear, but it wasn't easy, for when our country calls, we go. Yet the call to stay with the Girl Scouts was even more powerful because I saw the forces at work in our society that were going against the healthy growing up of our girls, and I needed to respond. Listening to the spirit within, or what I call the whispers of our lives, is very important. When we ignore them, our lives are diminished, and we never reach the levels we could in understanding ourselves, our fellow travelers, our friends, even our families. Often, these whispers are telling us to say no to things so that we can reach our full potential and achieve what we are called to do.

The Power of No for Organizations

The Power of No is just as important for organizations as it is for individuals. Without the Power of No, the mission of the organization can become obscured by initiatives and programs that do little more than add clutter. Keeping the Girl Scouts mission focused meant that we had to use the Power of No on a regular basis.

As CEO of the Girl Scouts, I was in a position where, because of the cookie sales and the power of that army of girls going door-to-door selling cookies, I would occasionally receive very lucrative offers from businesses that saw those girls as an army of little super salespeople. A business leader would call on me and offer an astounding amount of money to the Girl Scouts if we would just have the girls deliver the company's brochures as they sold their Girl Scout cookies. Although the money would have been helpful, having Girl Scouts deliver promotional material for a private company had nothing to do with our mission. I would express appreciation for the offer and then explain that we were mission focused and that the business's proposal was not congruent with our mission.

One executive protested. "But the girls sell cookies all over the place!" "The cookie sale," I explained politely, "is part of a program for girls. It's not a promotion for a product."

Many, many years ago, the cookie sales program started with the Girl Scouts baking their own cookies at home and selling them to their neighbors; the money they earned stayed with the troop. Eventually, as the program grew over the years, commercial bakers were contracted to supply the cookies. By the time I left the Girl Scouts, we had seven bakeries at three companies supplying cookies, and the program was generating a third of a billion dollars a year. Even then, that money didn't come to the national organization; it stayed with the local councils and the troops. This was also a program where girls learned skills. They learned about the customer and what they valued. Little girls were learning how to speak to a customer, how to tell their story and the story of the Girl Scouts. They learned what customers wanted, how to take orders, and then how to deliver the cookies, knowing that when you make a promise, you have to keep it. And they learned always to say "thank you."

The girls also learned other skills through the program, such as asset management and where to "invest" the troop's assets. When I was the leader of Troop 17 in the basement of the Second Presbyterian Church in Johnstown, the thirty little girls sold an enormous amount of Girl Scout cookies, and then *they* had to decide what to do with the money. During one of our last years together, when they were in high school, they decided they wanted to go to New York City and visit the Museum of Natural History and the Metropolitan Museum, ride the subway, and then take a train to Mystic, Connecticut, to sail on the eighteenth-century four-masted schooner, the *Joseph Conrad*. Who would have thought that these girls, in our big steel, big coal town, would have the imagination to plan such an adventure? The Girl Scout program and the cookie sale made it all possible. What they learned went far beyond marketing, beyond how to sell cookies.

The cookie sale was a program, not just a promotional effort, and we said no when necessary, to ensure that the organization would stay firmly focused on our mission. We received a lot of seemingly attractive offers that could have exploited girls, and we turned them down because they weren't right for them. The first question always had to be, "Would this be good for girls growing up?" It took some courage to turn down a large sum of money, which we could have used, but mission and values had to come first. Once you become mission focused, it actually doesn't take much courage to say no to offers that don't further the mission, however attractive they might seem on the surface.

The Power of No, when supported by passion for the mission and commitment to values, enhances the ethical performances of both the leader and the organization. The lesson of no is not negative; it is powerful and positive. This is a core principle that has helped define my life.

PART TWO

MY LEADERSHIP
JOURNEY

CHAPTER 4

MY MANAGEMENT EDUCATION

S ome leaders are leaders from the day they begin to walk. Others begin early in a conscious study of leadership and then start to "climb the ladder." There are many paths. Mine was a simple one that began with a promise, "On my honor, I will try . . .," made with girls then ten years old. My experience as a Girl Scout troop leader was a remarkable gift. I took the job for six weeks and ended up staying for eight years.

At first, I must admit, I thought being a Girl Scout leader was not for me, but a Girl Scout neighborhood chairman decided I was a likely prospect. She tried to recruit me several times. Each time she came to see me, I had a good excuse not to join. I did not want to take a troop—I was the mother of a little boy, I knew nothing about little girls, and so on.

But she persisted. One November day, she stopped by with a sad story about Girl Scout Troop 17. The leader had left for India to become a missionary, and the troop was about to be disbanded. Thirty little girls in the basement of the Second Presbyterian Church would be abandoned.

I relented and agreed to take the troop for six weeks until a "real leader" could be found.

Before my first troop meeting, I studied the history of the Girl Scouts and found a connection. I thought it fascinating that in 1912, eight years before American women gained the right to vote, a woman named Juliette Low founded the Girl Scouts in Savannah, Georgia. She exhorted the girls of this presuffrage era with the message, "Remember, you can be anything you want to be—a doctor, a lawyer, an aviatrix, or a hot-air balloonist."

Reading the history took me back to a day when I was in second grade. Our teacher had asked each of us in turn, "What do you want to be when you grow up?" I had just read a story about how airplanes were now carrying the mail. "When I grow up, I want to be a pilot and fly the mail," I stated. All the boys in the class hooted and howled. One big, tough boy shot back, "Who ever heard of a girl flying an airplane?" I quickly retreated. Had I known Juliette Low when I was in second grade, perhaps I would have tossed off the boys' ridicule and followed my dream.

Not only did I find appeal in the Girl Scout mission, which we would later distill to "To help each girl reach her own highest potential"; I especially liked the idea that the organization was global. I had never traveled outside the United States.

I read the Girl Scout handbook and, without any training, went to that first meeting in the basement of the church, unsure of what to expect. I introduced myself to the troop and announced, "I am your leader." No one ten years old was going to question that statement, yet I was very uncomfortable. That was the first and last time I pronounced myself a leader.

The Girls and the Team Approach

My thirty Girl Scouts had enormous energy and never-ending enthusiasm for the troop, the meetings, and the values—and that energy and enthusiasm were contagious. They were always eager to learn new things. I never said, "No, this is what we're going to do today." It was their troop. Instead, they decided. Now some call what I did (or didn't do) "empowering," but I thought of it as releasing the energy and the creativity of girls to make their own plans. It was all about shared leadership. The troop was divided into patrols. Each patrol had a young leader. (Later we would call this "the team approach to management.")

Troop 17 sold Girl Scout cookies far beyond expectations and then practiced asset management—deciding on how to use the proceeds from the cookie sale. With their decisions they expanded their own horizons, as I recounted in the previous chapter, with travel to new places: Mystic, Connecticut, for a week on the *Joseph Conrad*, a four-masted sailing ship; New York City to ride the subway and visit the Metropolitan Museum and the Museum of Natural History; and other great adventures.

During those years, we spent time at Camp Blue Knob, the Girl Scout resident camp on the second-highest mountain in Pennsylvania; later, quite a few of the girls went on to become junior counselors at the camp, furthering their leadership experience.

The girls came from varied backgrounds, and none were particularly affluent. It is so critically important at ages ten, eleven, and twelve to imagine that there is a bright future, one that pushes far beyond the old boundaries that society sets for people. Earning a Docent badge in our local public library, an 1884 Andrew Carnegie institution, was a profound experience for GS Troop 17, and it later inspired Shirley Stahl, one of our members, to become a professional librarian.

Years later, one of the girls would write, "When we met Leader Frances, we were 30 girls unsure of ourselves with little ambition to do more than get married and stay in Johnstown. When we graduated from high school, we all had high ambition and confidence. We had accomplished so much as a troop and as individuals. Leader Frances made a difference in every one of our lives."

Years before I knew who Peter Drucker was, I was learning the fundamentals of management and leadership, learning far more from the girls of Troop 17 and the experience of working with them than I ever could have imagined. The way they responded to the values of Girl Scouting made a difference for me. They taught me the importance of hope and confidence, the Girl Scout vision established by Juliette Low so many years earlier. In the compassion and energy of that circle of Girl Scouts, my family found a bonus. When we went troop camping on Blue Knob Mountain, my young son, Johnny, would go with us, and that little boy, an only child, soon had thirty big sisters who loved him. He too could be part of a larger team.

The self-confidence of my troop members was the strongest evidence of the priceless value of our shared experience. One day, when the girls were fifteen years old, I told them I had been asked to be chairman of the board of our Talus Rock Girl Scout council. I shared my concern about the time this additional role would take. They responded, "We knew you would be chairman someday." They were beaming with pride—not for what they could do, but for me. They continued, "You just come to the meetings as our leader. We can take care of everything in the troop," and they did.

At eighteen, the whole troop graduated from high school. It was the end of eight glorious years with emerging young leaders. I hear from a number of them today; they are still exuberant about the shared experiences of our team, Troop 17.

Carry a Big Basket

Not long after I had first introduced myself to GS Troop 17 in that church basement, I attended a training seminar for new Girl Scout troop leaders. There I met Rose Hawkins, who worked in a dress factory and later became our assistant camp director, a best friend who taught me a lesson that stays with me to this day.

When I mentioned to her that another new leader had complained that she was not getting anything out of our training course, Rose responded with words straight from her southern mountain wisdom: "You have to carry a big basket to bring something home."

I have never forgotten Rose's well-turned metaphor. Through all the years, I have carried many big baskets of different types, materials, and shapes. The small basket with its small vision, small scope, small expectations, and small impact is woefully inadequate. When we carry a big basket, what we bring home can change lives and build community. It can transform organizations and societies. In the end, it is we ourselves who are transformed.

Rose Hawkins, working in a dress factory, truly understood the value of learning. She saw to it that her two daughters received graduate degrees, and although she is no longer with us, she is one of my heroes. She and I both had small children in those early Girl Scout days, and I know that my son's exposure to Rose Hawkins, when he was a "junior handy boy" at our Girl Scout camp, enriched his life, as knowing her did mine.

The Door That Opened Over Lunch

I went on to chair the local Girl Scout council, joined the national board of the Girl Scouts of the USA, was chairman of the National Program Committee, and served on an international committee for nine years that met twice a year at a Girl Scout–Girl Guide center called Our Chalet, in Adelboden, Switzerland. Going to Our Chalet was not my first opportunity to travel outside the United States.

The first came in the 1960s when I was on the national board of directors, before I ever became the CEO, and I was appointed to be one of six representatives of GSUSA at the triennial World Conference of Girl Guides and Girl Scouts to be held in Greece. I had never been abroad before. (There were many parts of the world I was interested in but never thought I'd see.) I remember the Queen of Greece welcoming us. You could see the Parthenon from our meeting place. It was the most amazing experience. At the conference, I met three hundred women from all over the world—Africa, Asia, Europe, and Latin America—and everyone lived the Girl Scout Promise and the Law, sharing a common history tracing back to the original organization founded in 1912. At the end of the conference, the king and queen hosted us on a trip to Crete. While I was there, I went to a beautiful park where I saw a man sitting under a tree. He looked at me and my uniform, and seeing my GSUSA patch he said, with an accent, "You know Pittsburgh?" I said, "Yes, I was born seventy miles away in Johnstown." He said he was a steelworker in Pittsburgh, but that he had to come home, "because I love Crete." I told him I could see why. "I love Crete too." And as we sailed back to Athens, I smiled to think about that Pittsburgh steel worker, back home in beautiful Crete.

I still have pictures from that trip of us wearing our uniforms and berets and little white gloves, going up the stairs to our plane for the flight to Athens. I felt so privileged—privileged to be part of the Girl Scouts here in the United States and then part of our great World Movement.

Every country I go to, I look at the people and think, *They look like the kids I went to high school with in Johnstown,* because men came from all over the world to work in the steel mills and coal mines around Johnstown in the 1880s and early 1900s. Their descendents were the faces of the wider world. Thus Johnstown helped me feel at home wherever I went.

I loved being a volunteer and a national trainer of board members, and loved working with Girl Scout gatherings in our country and abroad—India, Thailand, Kenya, around the world. The mission, the values, the opportunities to serve as a volunteer locally, nationally, and internationally were a rich and fruitful part of my life. My husband and son were always part of the adventure and cheered me on.

Then one day in 1970, three business leaders in my hometown invited me to have lunch with them. One was the president of a bank, another the president of the United Way, and the third a business leader who chaired the United Way board. I knew all of them, but why were these three together? I had already agreed to chair the United Way campaign in the fall (the first woman in forty years to do so). They had recruited me. We were friends. Over lunch, one said, "We thought you would like to know that we have found the new executive director for the Girl Scout council." (The council had lost its executive director and was in serious financial difficulty.)

I replied, "How wonderful—who is it?"

They said, "You."

Shocked, I said firmly, "I'm sorry. I am a volunteer, and I would never take a professional job."

Their response: "That's too bad, for if you don't take the job, the Girl Scouts will no longer be part of the United Way."

Facing reality, I said, "All right, I will take the job for six months, we'll get the finances straightened out, and then we'll find a real executive." Thus I became the executive director of the Talus Rock Girl Scout council, which was the name of our local organization in 1970.

A month later, I realized that, for me, management was the great adventure.

The first day I walked into the office, under my arm were six copies of Peter Drucker's *The Effective Executive*, one for each staff member. I did not know Peter Drucker; I just knew that his philosophy was exactly what was needed for the governance and management of our Girl Scout council. His philosophy and vision were so right for the Girl Scouts that I thought he had written this book just for us.

There was a magic about Peter's writing. He wrote and spoke to us in elegant, spare language that connected and inspired us, and moved us into the future. The vision he held before us embraced us; we made it our own.

We had all of his books and his works. His philosophy gave us the courage to launch a quiet revolution, transforming that small Pennsylvania Girl Scout council. We developed circular management and had a great time using "managing in a world that is round" to ban hierarchy—building a richly diverse organization. The Drucker philosophy became our philosophy; it was totally consistent with our mission, our values, and our vision of the future. (We will look more closely at circular management in Chapter Six.)

Gone was the cold, austere command-and-control style of the old hierarchy. Alive and passionate were mission, values, people, accountability, and performance—the Drucker management system.

In four years, those remarkable volunteers and staff transformed the organization; we even built an amazing new strategic planning system we called "Five Steps to Effective Programs in a Girl Scout Troop," a planning tool that other councils purchased for the cost of making the copies.

As I mentioned, I had already been recruited to chair the United Way campaign when I became the CEO of the local Girl Scout council. Inclusion, diversity, and equal access continued to be essential parts of my new career, as they were of my life. When the time came for me to choose the vice chairman for the United Way campaign (this was the happy prerogative of the chairman), I chose Ernest Wadsworth, president of the United Steelworkers of America in Johnstown—a first for our city. The president of the United Way said that he would have to ask Bethlehem Steel, who was a great supporter of the United Way. Bethlehem Steel endorsed my choice.

Ernie and I made a great team, and with Bethlehem Steel's enthusiastic support, we mobilized the community in a way that had never been done before. Bethlehem Steel hosted our campaign kickoff luncheon, and that evening, the AFL-CIO and the United Steel Workers hosted a large kickoff dinner. Leo Perlis, the VP of the national AFL-CIO, came from Washington to speak at the dinner, and many women mobilized other women to support the campaign, fearing that a woman chairing the annual drive might not get all the support that men had received in the previous thirty-nine years.

The power of inclusion once again was evident. That year, our little town had the highest per capita giving of any

United Way campaign, and Ernie Wadsworth was the chairman of the next year's very successful campaign.

Four years later, I got a call from a large Girl Scout council in eastern Pennsylvania, Penn Laurel, and was asked to take their executive director position in York. That same week, my husband John, a filmmaker, writer, and editor, received a call from the governor of Pennsylvania asking him to come to Harrisburg to work with his new Artists in the Schools program. The two jobs were a thirty-minute drive apart. Providence at work.

It seemed that we were being called. John sold his communications studio; we rented our house; and off we went, with John working in Harrisburg with the Pennsylvania Council on the Arts, and the Girl Scouts in York and the Pennsylvania Dutch country for me. We split the difference and got an apartment halfway between Harrisburg and York.

When I left Johnstown, I carried with me written introductions from steel executives to industrialists in the new council area and cards from a bank president who had close ties with other bank presidents in the Penn Laurel council area. These introductions helped make it possible for me to recruit the chairman of the board of National Central Bank to the 1975 Girl Scout fund drive, resulting in a campaign that doubled the previous year's result.

Johnstown's Central Labor Council also wanted to be supportive, and they called labor representatives in York to let them know that "a real friend of organized labor" was moving to York and should be given their support. This support continued when I moved to the national organization in New York City.

One of my final acts in Talus Rock was to recruit Congressman John P. Murtha as the chairman for the 1975 – 76 Girl Scout Annual Fund Raising Dinner, which he did annually ever after. He teased me about my recruiting him to chair the Girl Scout dinner and then leaving town, but he remained faithful to Girl Scouting for more than thirty-five years, chairing the fundraising dinner each year.

What It Means to Belong

Early in 1976, when I was the executive director (CEO) of the Penn Laurel council in eastern Pennsylvania, there was a conference for all Girl Scout executive directors in our six-state region, and I was asked by my colleagues to speak on "what it means to belong." So I gave the following speech in early 1976. When I wrote "What It Means to Belong" for my Girl Scout executive director colleagues, I had no idea that one of us would ever be considered for the national executive director position. Considering that since the beginning of our sixty-four-year history there had never been a CEO chosen from within the organization, a change would be unlikely. The national position had been vacant for a year. To me at that time, New York was very far away, and Pennsylvania was forever.

Providence works in mysterious ways. I found myself in New York later that year, carrying with me the "What It Means to Belong" philosophy, the philosophy I shared with my fellow council CEOs only months before the GSUSA announcement of my new position.

❧

What It Means to Belong

"What does it mean to belong?" is a great question to ask an executive director in 1976, for we are living in the best possible times for the Girl Scout movement. Since 1912, we have been answering this central question, and our response to the meaning of belonging then, and now, is shaped by our own times.

The basic values, the verities of this movement, remain vibrant and untarnished by the turmoil of our times. The values of our movement are as fresh and essential today as they were when Lord Baden-Powell beamed in vivid prose his mission: a high sense of ethics, the ability to set goals, the excitement of commitment to a better future for mankind ... and a vision of a world neighborhood almost three-quarters of a century ago.

In the sixty-seven years since the launching of Girl Scouting in Savannah, no catastrophe, no world holocaust, no social or economic evolution has diminished the need for a movement based on serving God (however you worship), on serving one's country, and working for a better life for all people. With certitude, with the security of our Promise [On my honor, I will try: to serve God and my country, to help people at all times, and to live by the Girl Scout Law] and those values implicit within it, today's members, girls and men and women, strive to redefine our basic values in terms that give meaning and authenticity to their lives.

Because we are a product of our own culture and because we are shaped by societal forces, every force both positive and negative shapes our response to "What it means to belong."

Look at the thousands of communities we represent, torn by the crisis in the schools, crippled by institutional racism, confused by the changes in the family across our country.

Margaret Mead said recently, "by the early 1970s the doomsters were proclaiming that the family was dead. There were over 8,000 single-parent households, most of them headed by poorly paid women . . . . But the family is not dead." She states, "It is going through stormy times, and millions of children are paying the penalty of current disorganization, experimentation and discontent. In the process, the adults who should never marry are sorting themselves. Marriage and parenthood are being viewed as a vocation rather than as the duty of every human being. As we seek more human forms of existence, the next question may well be how to protect our young people from a premature, pervasive insistence upon precocious sexuality, sexuality that contains neither love nor delight."

And while Margaret Mead is painting her picture of the family in the late 1970s, from many studies come the alarming statistics of the impact of the disorientation of this decade upon young girls. Seven hundred fifty thousand teenage pregnancies in the U.S. in 1974. Every third pregnancy in the country involves a teenager. And in York, Pennsylvania, readers were shocked to see headlines in their hometown newspaper — "Nine-year olds seek birth control but teen deliveries soar." And a California pediatrician was quoted in the article saying, "We see kids 11 and 12 delivering babies, so we're not getting to them early enough," and she continued, "Girls must be educated. They have to learn to make decisions. We have to teach them early — from five and on — to think about why people have sex. Obviously, eight-and-a-half is too late if we are seeing them at nine."

Leslie Westoff in her article, "Kids with Kids," in the *New York Times Magazine* section tells us of a new trend, of more and more white, middle-class, teenage girls having babies out of wedlock — and keeping them, not giving them up for adoption. Few are prepared for what comes after.

More than 200,000 teenagers (85,000 whites, 121,000 blacks) gave birth to out-of-wedlock babies in 1974. And the numbers are rising. Between 1971 and 1974, there was a 32 percent increase in illegitimate births to white girls under fifteen, for black girls only a 3 percent increase. And today four out of five of these young white girls choose to keep their babies and raise them. And with all the social, the human problems that this epidemic in teenage pregnancies brings forth, few are more tragic than that of the battered child. Studies show that "Cases of child abuse, of battered and neglected children are closely related to the age of the mother."

There are no easy answers to the problems facing the American family — to the enormous problem of teenage pregnancy. And I have highlighted only a few of the powerful forces that are shaping the world which nurtures our Brownies.

Massive challenges face adults in Girl Scouting, but the opportunities match the problems. This is the best possible time to be alive, to be working where it counts, to be an executive director of a Girl Scout council.

Always there have been opportunities, but never before has the time been so right for our mission, never have the times been so right for an assertive and positive position on the values of Girl Scouting and the difference they can make in the life of a girl.

It is in our favor that we never tried to be the swingers of the western world, even when it would have been easy to succumb to the expediency of attempting to "run with the foxes and bay with the hounds."

We worked for desegregation, when it was not "in" to do so. We fought and still fight for equal support of a program for girls in male-dominated United Ways. We were proponents of equality for women before women had the vote. Our girls were reaching out in waves of international sisterhood across oceans not yet spanned by aircraft, to clasp the hands of girls on every continent. And in the sixties when we were called square by those who questioned our values, we acknowledged that we were square in exactly the same way the Peace Corps was square. Service, integrity, and caring are hard to put down. In 1912, Girl Scouting was "an idea whose time had come." In 1976, in a new and unexpected way, Girl Scouting again is "an idea whose time has come."

James Reston writes in the *New York Times* that maybe the voters in the early primary elections are trying to tell us something. "They have been very cautious and moderate. As Eric Hoffer says in his book *In Our Time*, 'They don't quite know what is happening to them, they are separated from the past, a different people in a different country.' Somehow Hoffer thinks 'they still believe in believing and they yearn for the values of the past.'"

Reston feels that voters apparently are asking "for simpler, more honest and more moderate men and policies." He says that it seems a strange comparison, that Charles de Gaulle held France together in its critical postwar years, not by telling people what they wanted to hear but by setting a moral example. During that crisis in the life of a nation, when you ask why the men and women of France always supported de Gaulle on the great issues put to a vote of the people, they gave a plain and human answer, particularly the women. "We don't quite know whether he is right or wrong, but we trust him," they said. "He is our regret—the symbol of values we regret we have lost. So we support him. We would like to believe in his values, even if we don't live by them."

There is something of this same yearning in this country and in communities across our councils. We are in a beautiful position, a unique position, with deceptively simple values that can give meaning to the lives of girls and adults, a program based on our devout belief in the worth of girls and women and the right of girls to grow and develop to their fullest potential, a program that brings human promise to a dark and tragic decade.

It may seem strange to you that I have chosen a controversial primary campaign to illustrate the new opportunities for this movement, but this is part of my daily job as an executive director—to observe the current trends and events and to find the implications for Girl Scouting. The trends are strong and identifiable, and this organization needs to be ready to speak more clearly than ever before of the truths, the values that we strive to live by, as we share our Promise with girls of the seventies. Wherever we look, we see crises, chaos, and a cynicism about the established institutions in our country. Even we, ourselves, within the movement, have fought what some perceived to be the actions of an uncaring and insensitive Establishment. Yet it is exactly these circumstances that form the most fertile ground for a renewal of Girl Scouting, a fertile ground for the battles that we must undertake with and for the young.

As our country moves into its two hundredth year, we are engaging in a great introspection, in a looking back, in a study of where we have been and where we are going. Events of the last two decades seem less attractive than the glories of the early years. Our citizens read the Bill of Rights, the Declaration of Independence and some of the less well-known writings of our founding fathers, and then look at what we have wrought in our own society. There are reams of articles and stacks of books on "where did we go wrong," "how did we lose our way," how did we lose that sense of purpose that made us the "last best hope of mankind"? Letters to the editors speak of the downfall of the Roman Empire and the corollary between those times and ours. To balance the scale, there must be those who write and speak of the other side of that dark coin.

This is the exhilarating obligation of those of us who lead in any way—whether a board, a staff, or a troop. The decade ahead offers a new kind of opportunity to this organization. A fantastic opportunity to beam the message that we have been beaming for sixty-seven years, articulating a belief that there must be a place in this society for an organization that bases its work on honor, integrity, service, in equality of opportunity, for reaching out to all girls.

We need to be assertive about these values which give meaning to our lives and have the courage to share them with girls, but freeing them as Donald Michael says, "to define them in their own image so as to give meaning to their lives." The outward witness to the values of Girl Scouting by our girls today may not be expressed as that first Savannah troop expressed them, but they will be authentic and essential, appropriate in the lives of girls today. Have we the courage to respond in ways that are equally authentic? Have we the courage to be the advocates of the new young?

When we are compiling our doom and hope list, or call it "force field analysis" if we wish, one of the powerful forces that is pushing us toward our goal is the present climate and opinion in this country. In a slick and cynical age, there is an emotion permeating this country, a yearning for simpler, more honest ways, a yearning for the values of the past to give meaning to the present.

Reston speaks of "the differences and controversies within a nation that has been battered by contention for a generation." We are part of that generation that has been battered by contention; we have served a generation of girls and families who have been part of that battering. And now Girl Scouting must answer the challenge of what it means to belong with a renewed sense of purpose, a sense of the indispensability of our program for girls.

A recent study of Madison Avenue advertising agencies concludes with the opinion that we are operating in a "decade of lost illusions and tight money" and that "the customer is hard to fool."

If advertisers are right when they say the customer is harder to fool, then it means the customer is asking questions about the product, whether it is soap or cigarettes. How marvelous that we can build on this consumer reluctance to be fooled and a new questioning of the product. You and I are in the position of having something the customer needs — not a gimmicky short-term, hard-sell, but a way for girls and families to cope and grow. We have a product, a way that has been tested by a long green line for years, ever changing in its outward expression, but ever giving light and depth and meaning to the lives of those who shared it.

Emerson wrote, "This time, like all times, is the best time if we but know what to do with it." I am looking at the executive corps of a region that was bisected but not divided by the Mason-Dixon line, that acted as a catalyst for the understanding of common concerns across the organization, and I see the corps of executive directors who care so deeply about this movement and its purpose and their work within it that they wished to begin this meeting with a look at what it means to belong.

Many times since I have been in Girl Scouting, we have been swimming against the tide, or at least perceived as swimming against the tide. Today I find myself, as an executive director, in a marvelously uncomfortable but exhilarating position. Our own times have moved us into a position where the very basic philosophy, the values of our movement are congruent with a great turning, a great searching within our society. We "have something for the girls," for their families and for communities across our land. The meaning of belonging, today, holds enormous promise for those in the caring and growing and nurturing business.

We may question many of the "how to's" of our organization; we may question some of the direction; we may question some aspects of our partnerships, but we hold dear the values which are the heart of this movement.

Mrs. Dora Lykiardopoulo of Greece, chairman of our World Committee, spoke to a world conference I attended in Athens on what it means to belong. May I close with her words—"We have promised to do our best and nothing can be better than to continue to serve young human beings entrusted to our care, who carry in them the immortal spark without which this world and this life are without meaning. In the midst of ceaseless flux, challenged by materialistic gospels, the spiritual values of our simple principles survive unblemished. This resilience reminds me of words written seventeen centuries ago about buildings still standing today as a *proof* of man's share in things eternal:

"They were created for all time, in a short time. Through their beauty they were already at their conception, ancient; but in their vigor they are to this day fresh and newly wrought. Such is the bloom of perpetual youth upon these works, that they look for ever untouched by time as though the unfaltering breath of an ageless spirit had been infused into them."

We thank our Founder.

CHAPTER 5

NEW YORK CALLS

We had all lived through the trauma of the 1960s and early 1970s. Some organizations lost their way. Others were bewildered as they faced the challenges before them. The Girl Scouts were not immune to the turmoil and problems in our society. With eight straight years of declining membership, the Girl Scouts were in danger of losing relevance as social changes remade America. The Girl Scouts were predominantly white, and although the organization was eager to reach out to all races and ethnicities, it was unsure how to do so. The girls of America had new problems and new aspirations. They worried less about preparing for marriage and more about college and careers, less about home economics and more about increasing pressure to have sex or experiment with drugs. They wanted and needed a highly contemporary organization that could help them become leaders in the world and responsible for their own lives. Yet the national executive director (CEO) position had been vacant for one year.

When the search committee looking for a new CEO for the national organization invited me to come to New York, I almost did not go, for if in sixty-four years there had never been a leader chosen from the field, why now? My husband

John said, "The job is exactly right for you. I am driving you to New York. I'm a filmmaker, I can live anywhere, and I've always wanted to live in New York."

I knew some of the people on the search committee from my time on the national board, and I liked them very much, but I doubted if they could be serious in considering a local council CEO. So in the interview when they asked me what I would do if I were to become the new CEO, I was very relaxed. I described a quiet revolution, a total transformation of the organization. The program had not been changed in twelve years, despite all the social changes in the society around us. We did not have a highly visible racial or ethnic representation in the field. We had the usual hierarchical structure, and the 335 local councils were quite distant from the national organization. It was not One Great Movement. On one island were the local councils, and on another island, the national organization. So the challenge was to work to build One Great Movement, serving all girls of every racial and ethnic group.

I knew that the practices of the past were not relevant to the present we were living and the future we envisioned. I knew that equal access, building a richly diverse organization, was an indispensable part of a demographics-driven, customer-driven future.

It was essential to move into a very different future. We knew we had to change, so I described the total transformation of a great movement. We would question everything—never the mission of serving girls, or the values one lived, the Girl Scout Promise—but all the how-to's. We would develop a highly contemporary program and build a richly diverse organization. The Girl Scouts had to be part of a bright future. We had to lead from the front in those very difficult times.

After I left the meeting with the search committee, John asked me how it went. I told him I had a wonderful time describing the organization of the future, with a great search committee, but that was it. They were "casting the widest net," I believed.

Soon there was a call. I was offered the position of national executive director, and on July 4, 1976, John and I watched the Tall Ships sail up the East River in celebration of the bicentennial from an apartment six blocks from Girl Scout headquarters at 830 Third Avenue. I had arrived in New York to become chief executive of the Girl Scouts of the USA, having left a small town in the mountains of western Pennsylvania to lead the largest organization for girls and women in the world. It was an organization of enormous complexity, with over three million members—650,000 men and women serving over 2 million girls and young women, 335 local chartered councils, a cookie sale grossing a third of a billion dollars every year. It was an organization of long history and proud tradition—a great American institution.

Choose Your Battles

I had just arrived in New York when we were confronted with a delicate issue that could easily have distracted us from the important work of transforming the organization. The Boy Scouts of America, who already had been recruiting fourteen-year-old girls to become members of the Explorer

73

Boy Scout troops, were running advertisements referring to "Scouting USA," with no mention of the name Boy Scouts. It became very confusing to the public. We had calls from people who had contributed to what they thought were the Girl Scouts, and the thank you was coming from the Boy Scouts of America.

So the Girl Scout chairman of the board (president) and I made an appointment to talk with my counterpart with the Boy Scouts and their legal counsel. We presented our case in their lawyer's office, and the response was negative. "There could be no misunderstanding on the part of the public ..." and so on and so on. We met with a total rejection of our concern.

We decided to choose our battles and not to waste precious time battling someone else's slogan. We chose to invest in the future of girls and young women. We passionately believed that there had to be an organization in our society designed to meet the very special needs of girls growing up in turbulent times. (It would be five years later in 1981 that we would meet Peter Drucker, who would tell board and staff the first time he met with us, "You do not see yourselves life size. You do not appreciate the significance of the work you do, for we live in a society that pretends to care about its children and it does not, and for a little while you give a girl a chance to be a girl in a society that forces her to grow up all too soon.") We would ignore the Boy Scout issue, focus on our own future, the future of millions of girls growing up in a period of massive change.

We concentrated on building a great organization, a movement designed to meet the very special needs of girls growing up today, reaching out to all girls, of all races and ethnic groups. We poured our energy into developing a highly contemporary program, providing the best learning opportunities for all of our adults, and building our own national conference center, activities that reflected the significance of the largest organization for girls and women in the world. We succeeded.

Inclusion

In 1976, the gatherings of corporate and organizational chief executives had few female faces. But some CEOs, and I was one of them, developed our own philosophy, our own style, and our own leadership language—instinctively banning the old hierarchy. I felt all of us were called to work together to transform the organization. We would become the organization of the future. It was a powerful call.

One of the most important parts of transforming a large and complex organization is *inclusion*: engaging all of the people every step of the way. You can't develop a great plan, "give" it to "the people," and expect them to feel that it's theirs. So every Girl Scout planning group and every working group had people from the councils, volunteers, staff, board members involved—so that decisions were everybody's business. When you include representatives of all of your people, you've opened a door, making people feel welcome. Even though the new transformation represented massive change, it was amazing how we all came together, because it was "ours."

People watch leaders very carefully. When we make a statement on mission or values, it can't be just the rote recitation of words on a plaque on a wall somewhere. When we say, "We manage for the mission, we manage for innovation, we manage for diversity," we must demonstrate what that means in action. Everything we do, every action, every initiative has to clearly express the values. Young people watch very carefully how we work with them. They watch every move. Our behavior must be consistent with the messages we deliver.

Our first priority was to develop a highly relevant and contemporary program for all girls. The program had not been changed in twelve years, so that was number one. We had to find out what was happening to girls and young women in our society. What were the trends that were affecting girls today? What was affecting a healthy growing up for all girls? What kinds of programs would meet their needs—not just what we thought was good for them? We never flew on assumption. We did solid research.

So when I said to our 335 local Girl Scout councils in July 1976 that in one year we would have four new handbooks with a highly contemporary program for girls ages six through seventeen, grouped into four age levels, I could see a few little smiles, because nothing happens that fast. I knew that in those past years it had sometimes taken a long time to keep promises. We had doubters who didn't think it would be possible to do the research, the writing, the testing, and the publishing all in twelve months. But we did it. Promise made and promise kept. Our members were inspired.

The goal of delivering a new, highly contemporary program in twelve months wasn't an initiative to impress our people: the need was great. Girls were facing enormous challenges to their healthy growing up, and here they were using handbooks and program materials that had been written twelve years before, for the world of 1964. Think of the enormous changes that had gone on in society during that period of great turmoil! We were now living in a different world! Change in the program was imperative.

The Girl Scouts were very active in meeting the challenge and opportunity of diversity. When I became CEO in 1976, the chairman of the board was African American. Dr. Gloria Scott was chairman of the board and head of the search committee that selected me. We had three women on the board who headed Native American organizations. The Girl Scouts had a history, long before I got there, of having very powerful women of color on the board, of having a richly representative staff. The Girl Scouts didn't just preach diversity; they lived it.

But I feared that the diversity of our board and staff was not reflected in the membership. When I asked our staff, "What is the percentage of our membership from America's racial and ethnic groups?" I was told that we didn't collect that information because it might be seen as discriminatory.

I said, "I think we might be discriminating if we don't." So we collected the relevant information and found that only 5 percent of our membership was from a racial or ethnic minority. We were not happy. Why weren't we attracting more girls from racial and ethnic minorities?

How did people in the five major racial and ethnic groups feel about us? How did the people in all the local councils feel about these groups they were not serving, and how could they bring them in? I knew we had to do solid research. So I went to see Vernon Jordan, who was then president of the National Urban League, and asked if his great researcher, Dr. Robert Hill, who had published *The Strengths of Black Families*, could do the research for us. We would pay his salary, whatever it would take. Vernon listened to my story and said, "If that is what you want to do, I'll give you Bob Hill."

Because it was solid research by one of the best researchers in the country, we felt very secure when we read the report which found that the people in these groups wanted us as much as we wanted them, but they didn't know how to access us. On the other side, local councils all over the country, in small towns and big cities, wanted to bring in girls and leaders who were black, Hispanic, Native American, and Asian, but didn't know how to begin.

So we did our research and engaged great educators in helping us develop new handbooks; then we went out and piloted the program. We had girls and leaders use the new handbooks. How did they like them? Did they work? The on-the-ground experience of girls and leaders in the troops would determine the relevancy of the new program. We never said, "We've been doing this since 1912; we know what is good for them." It was also important to us that the leaders, no matter what their background, no matter their educational level, had to see the new materials as a positive way to help girls learn and grow.

As we developed the new program, I asked to see the four artists, one for each handbook, and delivered my message: "When any girl in this country opens her handbook, I want her to be able to find herself." When one artist asked, "Did you say *any*?" I replied, "I should have said *every*! If I'm a little Navaho girl on a Native American reservation, I can find myself. If I'm a little girl in the inner city, I can find myself. The handbook cannot just be filled with New England white picket fences." The artists got it; in fact, they caught on fire.

So one year from the day we promised, with the help of four distinguished educators and four great illustrators, we had a new program and four new handbooks, focusing heavily on math, science, and technology. The girls and leaders loved the new handbooks and made them their own. Computer Fun became the most popular proficiency badge for girls.

Next came the challenge of moving our entire organization, which was 95 percent white, to become richly diverse. Using Dr. Hill's research and working with Dr. John W. Work III as our new consultant, we trained all of our people in diversity, in councils and the national organization, right across the organization.

We also developed exciting promotional materials for each group. We created posters featuring a leader from each cultural group in her Girl Scout uniform, with girls in her troop around her, set with a caption sensitive to the culture and values of each group. For Native Americans, our message was "Your Names Are on the Rivers." We learned that black Americans were proud of the way they helped each other; their poster read, "Black Americans Have a History of Helping Each Other." We learned from the research that

Hispanic families do not like people talking directly to their daughters, so the poster for Hispanic families stated, "Girl Scouting Has Something of Value for Your Daughter." We plastered these beautiful posters featuring "real live" troop leaders and their Girl Scouts all over the country. At the same time, we developed exciting videos and other supporting materials to help local councils use the new materials and move beyond the old walls.

Our council people now had the training, encouragement, materials, and recruitment plan. Out they went, and in the girls came. We more than tripled racial and ethnic representation across the organization. Our field across the country delivered a miracle. Life was exuberant. There was no reluctance. Everyone was on board. For the next eight years, Dr. John Work III was on retainer two days a month. Any council, any group could call on him. Our visual materials were richly representative, and we began receiving awards for our handbooks as the "best multicultural resources for young people." We had asked ourselves the critical question, "When they look at us, can they find themselves?" And we made sure the answer was a resounding "Yes!"

Promises made, promises kept.

Releasing the Human Spirit

Our second priority was to make the Girl Scouts of the USA the organization of the future. We took our people out of those rigid boxes of the old hierarchy and into the concentric circles of a flat, fluid, flexible structure and system I call circular management. Circular management released the energy of our people — released the human spirit. (I describe our restructuring activities in Chapter Six.) We learned to mobilize our people — more than three-quarters of a million adults — around the mission: our reason for being, why we do what we do.

Sometimes we fail to fully appreciate the power of mission and values and vision — and the power of language. There is something about a battle cry that mobilizes people. So I worked hard on the language until the answer came clearly, and it would be my message for the next thirty years: "We manage for the mission." I later added the indispensable companions for the journey: "We manage for the mission, we manage for innovation, we manage for diversity." This battle cry permeated the total organization; it became a leadership benchmark — a simple but powerful way to describe the management and the focus of a great institution.

This battle cry did not just describe what we did, but who were. Then and now I defined leadership on my own terms, after much introspection, as follows:

> Leadership is a matter of how to be, not how to do. You and I spend most of our lives learning how to do and teaching others how to do, yet it is the quality and character of the leader that determines the performance, the results. Leadership is a matter of how to be, not how to do.

This was my thesis in those early days; it is my thesis today. The power of language is indispensable on our journey to transformation.

81

When you share a vision of the future that everyone helps develop, it becomes theirs and it's real. Nothing was developed behind closed doors and then presented as a bright idea to our people. No, they were involved every step of the way. This kind of inclusion builds morale, confidence, enthusiasm, trust, and support. It's magic. If you don't practice the power of inclusion from the beginning, you'll never achieve the results your organization deserves.

I've been gone officially from Girl Scouting a long time, but I still say, "Best people in the world, the best organization in the world." It was the power of vision, of mission, of innovation, of inclusion, diversity, and respect for all people—and living the Promise—that propelled us forward. When you take the mission off the plaque, off the wall, and help it grow in the hearts and minds of your people so that you all can express it every day in your work, you're building the organization of the future.

In the next few chapters, I will discuss some of the other challenges and opportunities we faced.

CHAPTER 6

CHALLENGING
THE GOSPEL

I t takes courage to challenge the gospel. In 1912, Juliette
Gordon Low telephoned a friend, saying, "I've got something for the girls of Savannah, and all of America, and all
the world, and we're going to start it tonight!" That evening,
she assembled eighteen girls from Savannah, Georgia, for
America's first Girl Scout meeting. A courageous, visionary,
even revolutionary woman, Low believed that all girls should
be given the opportunity to develop physically, mentally, and
spiritually. Here was a woman who couldn't even vote in
her own country, yet who said to those first Girl Scouts,
"Remember you can be anything you want to be—a doctor,
a lawyer, an aviatrix, or a hot air balloonist." The Girl Scouts
of the USA exists today because one woman was willing to
challenge the gospel in 1912. For almost one hundred years
that long green line has marched through history, millions of
girls in a movement that helped them serve, learn, and grow,
responding to the challenges of their times.

When I came to New York in 1976, as the Girl Scouts hurtled into the future during a decade of massive change, I knew there was no time to negotiate with nostalgia for outmoded, irrelevant policies, procedures, and assumptions. Our turbulent times did not accommodate the neat and tidy, "the way we've always done it" strategy, or even "the Way." We had to challenge the gospel of the status quo and keep only those strategies, projects, and policies that were relevant in the future—relevant to those we led, those we served, and those who waited to be served. We needed to find the courage to practice what Drucker called *planned abandonment*, which means keeping mission, values, and vision—the soul of the organization—centered and aligned as we abandon the vestiges of the past that spell irrelevance in the future. We had to get our house in order, and this required developing leaders of the future, leaders of change, to lead our organization into the future.

In the late 1970s and early 1980s, the future called for effective, ethical leaders in every sector, at every level of every enterprise: not *a* leader, not *the* leader, but many leaders dispersing the responsibilities of leadership right across the organization. That meant that we had to challenge the gospel of the old hierarchy.

Circular Management

I've known for a long time that my work—my style of leadership and management—is inclusive and circular. For me, life is circular. Although the idea of dispersed leadership is widespread now, it was unheard of in the hierarchical organizations of that era. These organizations used the language of command and control, of climbing the ladder, of top and bottom, up and down. They exemplified the famous pyramid with the leader sitting on the pointed top, looking down as his workforce looked up. And for many years, the old hierarchy that boxed people and functions in squares and rectangles, in rigid structures, worked well.

But in that period of massive historic change, of global competition and blurred boundaries, the old answers did not fit the new realities. In all three sectors, there grew a new cynicism about our basic institutions. With government, corporate, and voluntary or social sector organizations trying to ride the winds of change, a different philosophy began to move across the landscape of organizations, and with it came a new language, a new approach, and a new diversity of leadership.

At the Girl Scouts of the USA, we took our people out of those tired old boxes of the hierarchical structure of the past and into a circular, flexible, fluid management structure of the future. (It's described on the Leader to Leader Institute Web site, in "Managing in a World That Is Round" and "When the Roll Is Called in 2010.") And we purged ourselves of the dead hierarchical language. We threw out up-down, top-bottom, superior-subordinate. Have you ever met even one young person who couldn't wait to be a "subordinate"? We developed leaders at *every* level, and we discovered that circular management liberates the energy of our people, liberates the human spirit. (See the figure "Circular Management.")

Circular Management

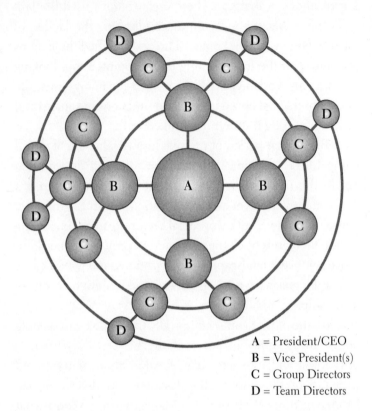

A = President/CEO
B = Vice President(s)
C = Group Directors
D = Team Directors

Circular management took care of the old barriers, and banning the hierarchy brought new appreciation for differing perspectives. Inclusion had many meanings, all of them helpful. The story of Troy is one example.

I always spent time with groups of new national staff members during their orientation sessions, meeting and sharing with them the mission of the organization, the values, and the significance of their work—our shared vision of the future—and then had all group members participate in the dialogue.

At one session with about eight new staff members, I asked each to introduce himself or herself and his or her position. One by one they spoke, telling us who they were and what they did. "I am Mary Smith, and I am the new computer specialist." "I am Charles Jones, and my job is marketing for national services." Then we came to the last person, a young man from the mail room.

He said, "My name is Troy. I work in the mail room, and I like to think of myself as the heart of the organization. Everything that comes into the organization comes through me. Everything that goes out of the organization goes out through me. I am the heart of the organization!" Troy's "heart" brought to us new insight about the importance of every person and every position. I've never forgotten Troy and that moment.

Inclusion is a powerful value: when we open up the organization, dispersing the leadership, including people from across the enterprise, there is a new energy, a new synergy. The old boxes communicated separation and could never provide the inclusive mind-set and "managing in a world that is round" that moves us to new levels of engagement, inquiry, performance, and results.

Transforming a Large and Complex Organization

We were committed to the transformation of a large and complex organization: we had to look at the structure, the position descriptions, and the kinds of support provided by the regional offices. We created working groups that included all those who would be affected as well as those sharing final responsibility. In two years, we completed a total reorganization of the GSUSA. Yet thanks to the power of inclusion and everyone's recognizing the essential nature of the change, the reorganization was accepted enthusiastically because it expressed a compelling vision of the future—and it *belonged to all*.

We examined our field structure, which at the time comprised six geographically based regional offices supporting the local councils in their regions. We decided to replace these six offices with three regional centers based not on geography but on demographics. The large metropolitan councils, for example, had different needs from those in widespread suburban rural areas. So we developed regional centers based on demographics, not geography: one for the large urban councils, one for smaller urban councils, and another for the smaller or rural councils, located in Chicago, New York, and Dallas.

Later, it became clear that our services could be even more effective if all of the field was served out of New York. So two years later, we decided to move all staff from the three regional offices to New York. Of course, this meant disrupting people's lives. To ease the transition, we said to the staff in each of those offices that all would have a job in New York—that every single person would have a job at a level and salary that he or she then held. And that took the heat out of it. Of course, there were some staff who didn't want to move to New York, and they were able to secure even better jobs with more money because of their experience with the Girl Scouts. That was one of the most gratifying parts of the whole experience: there was massive change, but people accepted it and, in time, even welcomed it.

Afterwards, the chairman of the Girl Scout national board said to me, "You could have moved everyone to New York in one step instead of moving from six regional offices to three, then all three to New York and taking two years to do it. Instead of doing it in phases, you could have brought all the field staff to New York at one time." I said, "I think you're right, but I had to be sure." In this significant transition, there was tremendous goodwill. The people in the regions knew how much the organization respected them, once again demonstrating the power of inclusion.

What happened along the way was a real coming together. Years earlier, there had been a disconnect: people would say, "We're local; they're national," some of them pronouncing "national" with a snarl, as if it were a mean word. All the while, I kept calling us "one great Movement serving girls," and after a while my language started coming back to me. As I was leaving the Girl Scouts, I received a moving letter from the CEO of a local council; she wrote, "I want you to know that on my wall, I have a plaque that reads, 'We are one great Movement serving girls.'"

Recently, speaking to many conferences of large national organizations with local affiliates, I have observed a renewed interest in seeing the total organization as a movement, appreciating the movement as more than local units delivering services to the customers on the ground, with the national organization providing resources, a national voice, and advocacy. Serving as chairman of the Volunteers of America, chairman of the Leader to Leader Institute, and

CEO of Girl Scouts of the USA, I have learned firsthand how the power and influence of a great national or international movement goes far beyond the efforts of an organization separated by levels, tradition, or an us – them mind-set. An effective movement unleashes new energy and generates trust, cohesion, and results that the old perceived separation of local and national groups cannot provide. One great Movement, mobilized around mission and changing lives, powered by circular engagement, leaves the old hierarchy behind and sends a powerful message for the future.

Managing the Transformation

It had taken almost two years for the volunteers and staff of Girl Scout councils and the national organization to consider every aspect of the transformation of our organization, and in late May 1978, we now were ready to bring together the management of the organization—the executive directors of all the Girl Scout councils, along with one hundred national staff members—for the presentation of the new Corporate Management Plan, which defined GSUSA's systems, structures, and delivery of services. The plan represented a powerful and passionate vision of how we were going to take the lead in this society. The Promise and Law, the values, the soul of the organization remained untouched, as powerful in 1978 as they were in 1912.

The participants at this meeting, the key staff members of the councils and the national organization, were coming together to study the plan, buy into it, and make it their own, for they were the staff leaders who would have to manage this massive transformation, to implement this Corporate Management Plan for the future of the organization.

My management team and I were prepared to take the lead in this pivotal presentation. The national board had approved mission and goals. This was management's response.

On the last Monday in May 1978, five hundred Girl Scout executives were gathering at a conference center in New Jersey to discuss the presentation. I was not there, but in a hospital in Manhattan, beside the bed of my husband John, who was dying of a massive malignant brain tumor. He had been in a coma for weeks and was now brain-dead.

At six o'clock that morning in a little kitchen off the intensive care room, I audiotaped a short message to our wonderful staff from all over the country who would be at the conference, sharing my appreciation of them and my anticipation that together they would make the decisions best for girls, best for our one great Movement. I told them that John was dying, and asked for their prayers.

Ruth Boyd, a member of my corporate management team, arrived. I gave her the tape with my message and asked her to play it as they opened the conference. She handed me the agenda the seven of us had so carefully prepared—each of us playing major roles in the presentation—and said, "Please tell me how you want us to handle your part in the three days." I replied, "You and our team will know. You make that decision."

So on that Monday, the five hundred staff members from all over the country and our New York headquarters gathered, my message was played, and my management team kept the faith. They led a powerful meeting that launched the transformation of Girl Scouting in the U.S.A.

It seemed that the tragic death of a good man, one very much a part of our Girl Scout family, added a sobering dimension to the deliberations of those three days. Some who came to the conference perhaps with the intention of challenging parts of this massive change shared with me later that John's death gave them a broader perspective, and somehow the tragedy of death and separation brought the participants closer together. Even in death, John could heal and unify.

On Wednesday, their last day together, I sent word that John had died. On Friday, my management team traveled to Johnstown for John's viewing, with Dr. Gloria Scott, who chaired the national board of directors.

It is strange for me to remember that at first I was reluctant to think about leaving Pennsylvania, whereas John felt passionately that the New York move was exactly right for me, for us. The two years we spent together in New York were two of the happiest years of our marriage, and then John was gone. My contribution to the Girl Scouts and to the Drucker Foundation (Leader to Leader Institute), whatever it has been, is part of his legacy.

I often think about our early years in Johnstown when diversity, equal access, inclusion, and respect for all people were part of our family and business ethic. John's courage, his example, gave me the confidence to make those values part of my leadership journey—up to this very moment.

CHAPTER 7

BECOMING A
CHANGE AGENT

Peter Drucker celebrated his ninety-third birthday with a seminal article in the *Economist* magazine, "The Next Society—Survey of the Near Future." Peter's wisdom is spread across twenty incredible pages. I keep it on my desk. He wrote,

> To survive and succeed, every organization will have to turn itself into a change agent. The most effective way to manage change successfully is to create it. But experience has shown that grafting innovation onto a traditional enterprise does not work. The enterprise has to become a change agent. It requires the exploitation of successes, especially unexpected and unplanned-for ones, and it requires systemic innovation. The point of becoming a change agent is that it changes the mindset of the entire organization. Instead of seeing change as a threat, its people will come to consider it as an opportunity.

Although Peter had not yet written these words in 1976, I had devoured all his books, and realized that the Girl Scouts of the USA had to become a change agent, and that meant changing the mind-set of the enterprise.

Life-Size Learning

Learning is a passion for me. I still remember my first day of school. My teacher, Miss Alice Jones, passed out our first book, a reader. I was so excited. I had learned to read before starting school. She told us, "Open your books, and we will read it together, one page at a time." I was so thrilled with my new book that I started reading page after page, forgetting what Miss Jones had told us. I looked up, and my teacher was standing in front of me. "Did you forget what I said about reading the book, all together, one page at a time?" she said as she took my book away from me. Miss Jones gave it back to me the next day, but how I suffered those twenty-four hours. I had disobeyed my teacher, and I had lost my book. Lesson learned: experience learning every day of your life, but listen to your teacher.

Just as individuals need to learn, so do organizations. Organizations that are slow to learn are slow to adapt and change. When I arrived at the GSUSA, our first priority was to develop a highly contemporary program to meet the needs of the girls who were our customers, as I recounted in Chapter Five. This in itself required us to learn and change so that we could move ahead and become the organization of the future. But further, our second priority was to make the Girl Scouts a *learning organization* so that it could *continue* to meet the evolving needs of girls in the midst of social change.

Girl Scouting is not just a program. It's life shaping, preparing girls and young women to move into a world that exerts very negative forces against a healthy growing up. So it was and is important to stay current and relevant by studying what is happening in the environment, and identifying trends that are emerging. If you can identify emerging forces, prepare for them, and have a program ready before they hit, you are light-years ahead of where you would be if you waited for the impact. It is the continuing study, the research into what is just over the horizon, that places the board and staff in a very positive position to help everyone in the movement be part of that future and not just react to it. We invested heavily in the training and development of our people, and the money was peanuts compared to the results. The first item in your budget should be learning, education, and the development of your people.

We always had our slogan, "Only the best is good enough for those who serve girls." One of my priorities was to modernize the Edith Macy Conference Center, which was far from "the best." The original Edith Macy Training Center opened in 1923. It had platform tents, and distinguished women from all over the country would come there for training sessions. Their motto was "We come together and we learn." Over the years, women decided they didn't want to live in tents to learn, and attendance at the center had declined. So, with the enthusiastic backing of the board and staff, I recruited John Creedon, the new president of MetLife, to lead our fundraising campaign, which raised $10 million for our new Edith Macy Conference Center on four hundred idyllic wooded acres in Westchester County, just forty-five minutes from New York City.

When it was completed in the early 1980s, the conference center was everything our leaders deserved. It was symbolic of where the organization was headed, yet also maintained our tradition of coming together and learning. We could house two hundred people in comfortable rooms, bringing them together for training sessions and conferences.

On the day the new conference center opened, the first sessions were for Girl Scout troop leaders—leaders from all over the country. I was there to greet them. One of them said to me as she looked at the beautiful auditorium, "I knew it would be nice, but I didn't dream it would be this nice." To me, her expectations indicated that she didn't see herself life size, or perhaps didn't see the Girl Scouts life size. But a week later, I saw her again as she was leaving, and her confident new spirit was obvious. She came up to me to talk about her plans and told me how she was going to share what she learned when she got back home.

We had great leaders like Peter Drucker, Warren Bennis, and John W. Gardner work with us, and what they and our new center did to help the whole organization learn, develop, and grow was deeply fulfilling. All these great thought leaders were so excited by the transformation of the Girl Scouts and what we were achieving that they were pleased to be part of the process. They came and spoke for us, trained our people, and did it for free as their contribution to the future of the Girl Scouts.

Every September, I brought our council CEOs together at Macy for a conference we called "Adventure in

Excellence," with Peter Drucker and other thought leaders. These sessions were an amazing part of making us a growing and learning organization. If we didn't see ourselves life size—a term we learned from Peter—when we began, we certainly did along the way. Preparing to come to Macy for our Adventure in Excellence session, participants would receive a book bag with several books. When they arrived at Macy, the authors of those books were there waiting for them. It made people feel that they were doing significant work for an organization that changed lives, that they were professionals doing professional work, whether paid or unpaid—life size.

Now with all the remarkable change in minds and hearts, as I worked with our local council CEOs, my local counterparts, the indispensable team, I observed that some still did not see themselves life size. How could we change these minds? If they could not see themselves life size, how could they see the organization and its future life size?

So two-and-a-half years into the transformation, we went to the Harvard Business School to talk to Dr. Regina Herzlinger about the possibility of a team of Harvard Business School professors developing a corporate management seminar for Girl Scout executives. Dr. Herzlinger, with Dr. Jim Heskett, Dr. James Austin, and others, designed a very powerful executive development seminar for all the local council CEOs and national staff members.

Our people participated, fifty at a time, until all had completed the Harvard Corporate Management Seminar for Girl Scout Executives. Each received a Harvard certificate to hang in their offices, along with new spirit, new appreciation, and high motivation—life size.

When you offer this exposure to great academic leaders in a perfectly designed leadership development opportunity, you ignite a revolution of rising expectations. Our Girl Scout leaders were eager for more and asked, "What's next?"

These local CEOs were responsible for a cookie sale that generated a third of a billion dollars every year, funding hundreds of conference centers, camps, headquarter buildings, and the essential supporting budgets. So "What's next?" became Dr. Herzlinger's Asset Management Seminar—an enormous contribution to the effective financial management of the organization. This investment on the part of a team of Harvard Business School professors contributed heavily to our success. Over five years, membership soared—the adult workforce grew from 650,000 to 788,000, and racial-ethnic membership more than tripled.

What was one of the indispensable ingredients in this massive transformation of the Girl Scouts of the USA? It was the major investment in the leadership development of our key professional leaders, and having the best business school faculty in the world partner with us. An interviewer once asked me, "What led you to choose Harvard Business School faculty?" I replied, "It is very simple; only the best is good enough for those who serve girls."

Get Feedback

Part of learning is getting feedback. But how do you measure your development as a leader? You may think you are a great leader, but those around you may have very different opinions.

In 1982, a young man named Marshall Goldsmith walked into my office at Girl Scout headquarters in New York with a great and revolutionary idea, a process, an assessment tool designed to help every staff member become better: 360-degree feedback, in which a person's peers and others all rate that individual's performance in specific categories. This process is well known today, but in 1982, no one else was doing this or talking this way, and here was this stranger presenting a great gift. He offered to use the tool personally with our national staff, conducting an assessment of their performance with confidential input from their coworkers.

I was very impressed with Marshall and the new concept, accepted the contribution with great appreciation, and made plans. We would begin with my management team of six, and Marshall himself would begin with me, so that the team would see the process not as something being done to them but as a total staff development experience. We all were going to participate, and the national executive director would go first. It was a powerful experience that changed the way we looked at ourselves, our fellow workers, and the organization.

We moved Marshall's 360-degree feedback process, which he later named "The Girl Scout Leader of the Future," across the organization, and trained staff as facilitators. It had a tremendous and continuing impact on the growth and development of our staff. Marshall and I became partners for life.

In 1990, Marshall became a founding board member of the new Peter F. Drucker Foundation for Nonprofit Management, now the Leader to Leader Institute. Marshall writes for us, speaks for us, and is coeditor of our "Future" books: *The*

Leader of the Future (1 and 2), *The Organization of the Future (1 and 2)*, and *The Community of the Future.*

We talk every week and join twenty-five great thought leaders of his Leadership Network every January, and if I call him and say, "Marshall, can you go to Poland [or West Point, or anywhere else]?" his reply is always, "When do we leave?"

Respect Feelings

Change can be very difficult for people, particularly when the change will affect something they cherish. One example was our decision to modernize the Girl Scout pin and logo.

There came a point when the Girl Scouts had to look at the 1912 Girl Scout pin. We loved and cherished it, a trefoil with an eagle and arrows, but it didn't seem symbolic of our organization and of girls in the early 1980s. The Boy Scout pin was similar, also a trefoil, and the Boy Scouts had begun their ambiguous Scouting USA promotion, which many thought included girls. The traditional pin no longer symbolized the Girl Scouts of the future. All in all, we decided the time had come to change.

We went to Saul Bass, who at that time was the greatest graphic designer in the world. He had created the corporate image and stunning logos for numerous companies, including United Airlines, AT&T, Minolta, Esso, BP, and Continental Airlines. (Saul was also a leading title designer in Hollywood, working on such films as *The Seven Year Itch*; the Hitchcock films *Vertigo, North by Northwest,* and *Psycho*; and Steven

Spielberg's *Schindler's List*.) He was delighted to respond to our charge; he designed a beautiful gold trefoil (the same shape), but instead of the traditional eagle, against a green background were the faces of three girls, obviously female, obviously diverse, in profile, facing the future.

The Traditional Girl Scout Pin	The New Girl Scout Pin

When it was time to unveil the new design at our triennial national council meeting, which brought together several thousand leaders from all the local Girl Scout councils and the national organization, Saul himself introduced it. He gave a beautiful presentation of the meaning of symbolism throughout the ages, discussing heraldry, flags, and other symbols, and how powerful symbols can be. Then he displayed the new pin design and described it in his powerful language: female, diversity, future. This was not the symbol of the organization of the past; it was the symbol of our future.

A large number of members were determined to vote down the new design. They were devoted to the 1912 pin. After Saul Bass made his presentation, I followed, saying in a soft voice, "From now on, this will be our service mark, our Girl Scout pin, our logo we will be using on all of our materials, but I promise you, as long as there is one person among our three-and-a-half million members who wants to wear the traditional pin [I did not say "old" but "traditional"], we will continue to manufacture it. You have my word." And that took all the heat out of the potential conflict. No one would be forced to wear the new pin; it was only for those who wanted to make the pin part of their work. A majority of the Girl Scout councils decided to adopt the new pin. We felt we were on a powerful, accelerated, successful journey into the future, and a majority of our people agreed that the new symbol was part of that future.

But we respected the feelings of those who did not want to change. I talked to one woman who was wearing the traditional pin; she put her hand over her heart and the pin and said with great feeling, "My grandmother wore this pin!" And I replied, "I'm so grateful to your grandmother, and I'm so grateful to you." There was never any pressure to make people change to the contemporary pin. We never said, "It's part of the past." With respect and appreciation, we moved into the future with our new symbol.

Timing Is Everything

When does the sled take off? is the question for all leaders, knowing that we can fail if the sled leaves too early with too few people on it, or we can wait too long, and someone else will have filled the need and eaten our lunch. It takes managerial courage to decide the right time for the sled to take off—blasting into the future with a new initiative, a new program.

Some people may oppose an initiative. As a leader, you need to respect their opinions and positions, but cannot be deterred by this. Later, many will change their minds and join you, but not if you acted in a punitive way that diminishes them. They will never come back. And this is a key principle in managing change, in mobilizing your people around change: give them time to adjust, and respect their opinions.

An example that lives with me as an exciting and well-documented case of knowing when the sled has to take off is our initiating the Daisy Girl Scouts program.

It was an exciting time for the Girl Scouts of the USA. We had increased membership, increased diversity around the country in our local councils, and provided a highly contemporary program for girls. We were truly one great Movement. Then a small group of councils, only 70 out of 335, came to us with a request for a new program for five-year-old girls. They told us that families, troop leaders, educators, community leaders—all the people who care about children—were saying that five-year-old girls were ready for a group experience such as that provided by the Girl Scouts. Families who already had daughters in the Girl Scouts had younger daughters who they felt needed the Girl Scouting experience as well.

Instead of waiting to see if more councils would step forward with the same request, we told them we would study their request and respond. We went to the greatest child development researchers and educators in the field and asked them if they believed five-year-olds were capable of participating in a group experience such as the Girl Scouts could offer.

They did their research and came back with a resounding "Yes." Not only were girls this age ready: they needed and could benefit from it. There were no negatives. So, feeling on very solid ground, we worked with key educators to develop a program for five-year-old girls that was educationally and psychologically sound, which we called the Daisy Girl Scouts. Then we formed a number of pilot Daisy Girl Scout troops in local communities and videotaped the program in these pilot troops.

At our next triennial national council meeting we came prepared for opposition. We had heard "This is unsound," "We don't intend to be babysitters," and "How can a five-year-old understand the Girl Scout Promise?" We presented the Daisy Girl Scouts to the council leadership in session with a delightful tape of real, live Daisy Girl Scouts in a troop meeting. In it one Daisy Girl Scout with blond bangs and a little Daisy pinafore is asked, "What does the Girl Scout Promise mean?" She looks belligerently into the camera and says, "It means you don't hit your friends." (Peter Drucker saw this videotape and said, "If everyone understood that, it could be the first step to world peace.")

Everyone listened to the presentation, and at the end I said, "There are 70 of our 335 councils that need this program. Families and girls in their jurisdictions have expressed the need, so we are going to serve them. Those councils that want to be part of the program will send trainers to the July Daisy Girl Scout training, and in September we will launch the Daisy Scouts for the 70 councils that want and need this program. Any council may join later; it's absolutely not mandatory. For those who want the Daisy Girl Scouts, we will provide the new age level." This approach, respecting the dissenting opinions of our people, took the emotion out of the debate. With seventy councils on board, we announced that the sled was going to take off.

By July, 225 councils had signed up for the training. In a couple years, the people who resisted most behaved as though they had invented this highly successful program. As I noted earlier, the question for leaders is, How do you know when the sled should leave? It takes managerial courage to decide that it is time for the sled to take off when many are hesitant to climb on board. A leader respects their opinions and their positions, but cannot be deterred by them. Later these people may change their minds and join you, but if you act in a dismissive way that diminishes them, they never come back. *Save the face and the dignity of the people who oppose the initiative.* That is a key principle in managing change and mobilizing people around that change.

As we look back, the Daisy Scouts program seems like the obvious development, yet at the time, it seemed revolutionary. In fact, the new program became one of the most relevant and successful in Girl Scouting, and in a few years there were Daisy Scout troops in every part of the country. It was a beautiful example of the power of inclusion and of choice: we presented the idea and explained how it would be developed, who would develop it, and when it would be made available. Most important, we said that only those who see value in it and want to use it will participate. Those who do not want Daisy Girl Scouts are free not to accept the program. By not being forced, by being voluntary, the program became totally acceptable. What could have been divisive turned out to be an exuberant coming together. It was an illuminating moment in the long history of the organization.

Lessons Learned

- Listen to the customer. Focus on needs, not your own assumptions.
- Do your research. Recruit the best authorities in the field. Don't assume that people today have the same needs they did ten years ago.
- Prepare the groundwork—pilot-test the initiative on the ground, where the results will be achieved.
- Include everyone in the development, testing, and consideration of your idea or program.
- Lead from the front rather than push from the rear.
- Respect differences of opinion, yet move ahead when the call is clear.
- Know when the sled should take off. Wait too long for everyone to get on, and the moment is lost.

CHAPTER 8

FINDING OUT WHO YOU ARE

Sometimes the change we are managing rears up and grabs us by the throat. At a time of crisis, we find out who we are. Either everything that has happened in our lives has prepared us for the trial, or it hasn't. Can we keep our heads? Do we know what we stand for? Can we stay true to our values? These are just a few of the questions a crisis will answer, one way or another.

One night in the 1980s, while attending an Aspen seminar in Sacramento, I received a call from our national headquarters. A man had walked into a television station in St. Louis and claimed to have found a pin in a Girl Scout cookie. He was seen by millions holding the pin and saying, "I found this pin in a Girl Scout cookie."

"Where is the box?" he was asked.

"I threw it away."

"Where is the cookie?"

"I ate it."

There was only this one man's word, unsupported by any evidence, yet the television station put him on the air.

By the next day, six additional pins were found in cookies. Before the crisis was over, more than three hundred pins turned up in cookies from Alaska to Miami. Kids found pins, mothers found pins, all kinds of people found a pin in a Girl Scout cookie. And our Girl Scout councils were right in the middle of the annual cookie sale that provided a major part of their support.

I left Aspen immediately and at 9:00 the next morning held a meeting with our lawyers; our public relations firm, Burson-Marsteller, including the president and the public relations representative who had advised Johnson & Johnson in the Tylenol crisis; our management team; and our own public relations people. This was the message we crafted: "This is not a national crisis. We will treat each pin as an isolated local incident. We will not stop the cookie sale." We immediately put our senior executives on the telephones to respond to the public and to our own people. I was advised not to speak to the media until the FDA had inspected the seven factories in the country that baked our cookies and determined that the problem was not in the manufacturing. We were in constant contact with our local councils, who were managing the cookie sales.

When the crisis hit, I remembered how well James E. Burke and Johnson & Johnson handled their Tylenol crisis. When it was over, Jim Burke was an icon and Johnson & Johnson a celebrated corporation. His was a case study of what happens when a great corporate leader—guided by the beliefs and values that define the culture of a great corporation—communicates with clear and forthright messages, reassuring the public and the people of the corporation. Today, despite predictions at the time that Tylenol was a fatally wounded brand, it is still one of the top-selling over-the-counter drugs in the country.

I called Jim Burke at Johnson & Johnson and was put through to him immediately. I explained our "pins in cookies" crisis and asked for his advice. He was wonderfully responsive, offering to send to New York his two vice presidents who had managed their Tylenol crisis. Then he said, "Who is the public relations representative handling your case?" When I told him, "Tony of Burson-Marsteller," he said, "You don't need us. He's the best there is, but we are ready to help you in any way." We never had to call Mr. Burke, but it was reassuring to know that a great corporate leader was also a great example of corporate social responsibility.

Almost all councils continued their cookie sales, as we advised. Three days later, the FDA came back and said the problem was not in the manufacture or the distribution of the cookies—that the pins appeared only after the customer had received the box of cookies. At that point I could say authoritatively to the media that the pins in the cookies appeared after the boxes were in the customers' hands. The FBI set up Operation Stickpin and investigated all three hundred plus incidents. Every one of them was found to be a hoax. When a few pins in Girl Scout cookies continued to be reported, the FBI announced on television that there was a fine of $20,000 and five years in jail for such a crime. No more pins.

The lessons for us were very clear. (1) We didn't try to manage the crisis in-house, alone. (2) We got the best public relations and legal advice and followed it; we didn't try to second-guess our advisers. (3) We had the courage to stay the course and didn't try to tinker with the plan. (4) We stayed close to our local councils, our leaders, and our girls. Today this experience is sometimes used as a case study in crisis management training on how to deal with product tampering.

Some people in the organization questioned my not speaking out immediately. I said, "I will not speak for three days; we are going to follow the advice of our public relations firm and our lawyers. I will speak only when we know the answer and have something to say." Staying silent was hard to do, but it worked.

As I said earlier, in a crisis we find out who we are. From my teen years on, I never had a sheltered life. I had a wonderfully rich family life, but I had to be part of the world quite early. Early losses and early responsibilities had a great deal to do with shaping what I would do later and how I would do it. The values we live, the people in our lives, the events we live through—these are what shape who we are and what we do when called.

Staying Cool

As I was going through some old papers, I came across a note from a Girl Scout council executive director, who had attended our last good-bye with 334 of her colleagues, dated November 1, 1989. Here is an excerpt:

> This note is to say thank you . . . . for the recognition
> you have earned for the organization as a viable force
> in this ever changing world stage—and the grace with
> which we can make that change. You exemplify the
> qualities of leadership I admire most: vision, tenacity
> and "coolness under fire."
>
> With affection,
>
> Kate

If you had asked me then which qualities of leadership my Girl Scout council executives would have identified, I would not have thought of "coolness under fire," yet I guess when you are the leader who is under fire, remaining "cool" serves as an important, essential message to your people. If the leader is cool, then it follows that the rest of us will remain cool as well. Coolness under fire is also part of Peter Drucker's admonition to "think first, speak last." No matter how well led the organization, it is difficult to manage a crisis unless "cool" is the way the message is delivered. When we appreciate that "communication is not saying something; communication is being heard," as leaders in a crisis we will find the language that our people hear, understand, appreciate, and make their own. One team, one message. Cool.

Prepare for the Unknown

Now, more than ever, examples of badly managed crises in all three sectors underscore the imperative of preparing for a crisis that may lie ahead—one that may never happen but even so must be anticipated by responsible, effective leaders.

Recent history provides too few outstanding examples of leaders who understood the imperative, who prepared the organization for the event, who instilled values that would support a powerful and ethical response, and who—when the crisis hit—led from the front and communicated in an open and powerful way. These rare leaders prepared when the sky was blue and took costly action—made a wise investment, actually—that protected the public and, in the end, the good name and the future of the enterprise.

Crisis management is not a discipline to be learned on the job, in the midst of the storm. Organizations that cope with crises well have their houses in order; they know what their values are and have a well-articulated mission everyone appreciates. They know why they do what they do. Crises can strengthen these organizations, even as they undermine—or destroy—those that do not know what they stand for. Even in a crisis, leadership is a matter of how to be, not how to do. Yet there are still steps that wise leaders undertake.

An example of powerful and successful crisis management came on September 11. The world watched firefighters, police officers, medical personnel, and rescue workers respond to the unimaginable disaster. Skills they learned and practiced in hundreds of different crises prepared them for the ultimate challenge. The many teams became one team, and their planning, preparation, passion, enormous courage, and total commitment inspired the country and the world. They gave us a supreme example of crisis management on a massive scale, and the lessons learned from their response to September 11 apply to whatever crisis leaders may face on any scale in any organization. Some of us who have had the uncoveted experience of managing a crisis in a complex and far-flung organization have learned from that experience that there are some essential steps to be taken, regardless of size or sector, long before disaster strikes.

A crisis management team needs to undertake a study of every possible crisis that could hit the organization, and develop a scenario for the response to each one. This process of study and development takes time and investment, but it is the best disaster insurance an organization can have. The information is kept in desks and on computers, in easy reach of every member of the crisis management team.

Once the plan is finalized, the training and preparation for implementation take place. Some organizations have the expertise within the enterprise to train and prepare their people for that dark day, should it come. Others may choose an outside consultant to assist in this essential management responsibility, the training of those who will lead the response.

Even though, as some of us have personally experienced, the crisis that hits is not on the carefully prepared list of possibilities, the principles are the same. The plan of action will work and the results prove positive, even if the crisis has a different face from all those we brainstormed.

When lightning strikes, mission, values, and integrity in managing and communicating will be the indispensable ingredients to a successful conclusion. Effective leaders know that communication within the organization and with all constituents is as important as those with the public and the media. They will communicate with integrity and openness, using messages consistent with their mission and values; and they will stay close to the customer, both internal and external, focusing on what the customer values.

Recent history, as well as lessons of the past, demonstrate that crisis management is a leadership imperative. Every dollar and hour spent in preparation, before the fact, is the essential investment required for future confidence, credibility, and relevance. Only months before the pins-in-cookies hoax exploded, we had provided crisis management training to our key volunteers and staff members—providential timing that paid off.

In sum, here are my steps to effective crisis management:

- Appoint a crisis management team.
- Brainstorm all possible crises that could hit the organization, along with the response required for each.
- Prepare a master plan everyone understands, a plan with clear delegation of responsibility.
- Designate the official spokesperson for the national organization.
- Prepare the field as carefully as headquarters—one team, one voice, one response. (At the local level, every unit selects its own spokesperson to carry the message communicated by the national organization.)
- Secure or activate the best public relations team and firm.

In the end, crises are tests of the quality and character of leaders, as much as they are tests of leaders' skill and expertise. Whether you like it or not, they will show you who you are.

CHAPTER 9

MY JOURNEY WITH PETER DRUCKER

F ive years after coming to New York, I received a letter from John Brademus, chancellor of New York University, inviting me to a dinner at the University Club to hear Peter Drucker speak. I knew I wouldn't be able to meet Drucker in that group of fifty foundation and large social sector organization presidents, but at least I would be able to hear him in person.

The invitation read, "5:30 P.M. reception." Now if you grow up in western Pennsylvania, 5:30 is 5:30; so when the evening came, I arrived on time, walked into the reception room, and found myself alone with two bartenders. I turned around. Behind me was a man who had just walked in. He said, "I am Peter Drucker." (Obviously, if you grow up in Vienna, 5:30 is 5:30.) I was so stunned that instead of saying "How do you do," I blurted out, "Do you know how important you are to the Girl Scouts?" He said, "No, tell me."

So I told him about how those remarkable 766,000 men and women (1 percent of which were employed staff), serving more than 2.2 million girls, had transformed the organization, and I said, "If you go to any one of our 335 Girl

Scout councils, you will find a shelf of your books. If you read our corporate planning and management monographs and study our management and structure, you will find your philosophy."

"You are very daring," Peter replied. "I would be afraid to do that. Tell me, does it work?"

"Superbly," I told him, adding, "I have been trying to get up enough courage to call you, ask if I may come to Claremont, have an hour of your time, and lay out before you everything you say the effective organization must have in place. We do. I want you to look at where we are and then talk to me about how we can take the lead in this society and blast into the future."

Peter said, "Why should both of us travel? I'll be in New York soon, and I'll give you a day of my time."

Before we met again, Peter studied us at the council level—on the ground where the girls and leaders were—as well as our circular governance and management, and declared us the best-managed organization in the country: "Tough, hardworking women can do anything." I wasn't sure about tough, but hardworking, yes!

In 1981, the great day for our meeting came. The national board and staff members were in the boardroom. I am sure they expected him to comment on the results of the past five years, for these remarkable people with their partners in local councils had transformed the organization using Drucker's principles. He stood before us and thanked us for permitting him to join us—then he completely surprised us. "You do not see yourselves life size," he said. "You do not appreciate the significance of the work you do, for we live

116

in a society that pretends to care about its children, and it does not." I wanted to rise and refute this, but could think of nothing to say. He continued, "And for a little while, you give a girl a chance to be a girl in a society that forces her to grow up all too soon." We took him seriously.

As Peter was leaving Girl Scout headquarters that first day with us, we were in the lobby of 830 Third Avenue — our own headquarters built by an earlier courageous board and staff. He turned to me and said, "I can tell a great deal about an organization from its building. In this building, the culture is palpable, with little tension and no meanness." I had never heard "meanness" used in that way. I often think of the simplicity and power of his observation, and how we tried to live up to it. "No meanness" has a poignant relevance in our world today.

That was the beginning of eight years of Peter Drucker's enormous generosity. He gave us two or three days of his time each year, studied us, talked with us, advised us, and wrote about us. "Frances Hesselbein could manage any company in the country," he told the *New York Times*.

He spoke at every national Girl Scout conference and inspired us to move beyond the walls and lead into the future. Peter was part of the well-documented transformation of the Girl Scouts of the USA.

Keeping the Faith

In September of my final year with the Girl Scouts, I attended my last Adventure in Excellence conference (described in Chapter Seven). Peter was our final speaker. The program listed this session as "A Dialogue with Peter Drucker and Frances Hesselbein." Peter and I were seated on the stage ready to dialogue when the facilitator said, "Frances, we've played a trick on you. This is not a dialogue; Peter Drucker is going to interview you." Imagine being interviewed by Peter Drucker before nearly five hundred staff colleagues in this last time together with our great leadership group.

The interview began and I responded, inspired and intimidated. It was a moment in my life I would keep close forever. Peter Drucker's last question—a question I had never thought about—made me pause: "Frances, when you leave the Girl Scout organization and they hang your portrait on the wall, there will be a little brass plaque below the frame. What will be the inscription on that plaque? What will it say of you?" I had never thought of such a thing, yet I heard myself saying, "I hope it says, 'She never broke a promise.'"

Peter said, "No. It will say, 'She kept the faith.'" I carry with me Peter's message from that evening long ago, that imperative I try to live by.

Today, Peter's voice is with me when, sometimes, I end a speech with "Ten years from now, may they say of you, 'The future called, and they responded. They kept the faith.'" People translate "keep the faith" in their own terms, in their own lives, as I do. (I have included the complete interview at the end of this chapter.)

Redefining the Social Sector

I want to focus here on Peter's work and his messages about the social (nonprofit) sector, for he redefined and brought new recognition and significance to the social sector as the equal partner of business and government. "Nonprofit simply defines what we are not," he said. Peter had redefined the nonprofit, voluntary sector as the "social sector," for, as he said and believed, "It is in this sector we find the greatest success in meeting social needs. Somewhere in this country, wherever there is a problem, whatever it is, a social sector organization has found a way to solve it."

He wrote a seminal article in the July-August 1989 *Harvard Business Review*, "What Business Can Learn from Nonprofits." Some were sure it had to be a typo before they read the article, which turned on its head the old view of the nonprofit sector as somehow the junior partner of business and government. But Peter said, "The best-managed nonprofit is better managed than the best-managed corporation."

He lived to see the vast proliferation of college and university nonprofit management programs—centers for social enterprise—hundreds across the country and the world. One last area of massive influence among the many I could list is his achievement in bringing business leaders to see the community as the responsibility of the corporation: "Leaders in every single institution and in every single sector ... have *two responsibilities*. They are responsible and accountable for the performance of their institutions, and that requires them and their institutions to be concentrated, focused, limited. They are responsible also, however, for the community as a whole."

One measurable result of Peter's profound influence across the sectors is that collaboration, alliances, and partnerships across the three sectors have become the powerful shared vision of effective, principled corporate leaders and their social sector partners.

On the fifteenth anniversary of the Drucker Foundation – Leader to Leader Institute, April 2005, we celebrated Peter Drucker's life and contribution at our Shine a Light dinner. The name Shine a Light was appropriate that evening and now, for that's what Peter did for ninety-five years before he left us, and still continues to do beyond his centennial. His light inspires young people just discovering his ideas; our young leaders of the future find relevance and inspiration just as leaders of the present find the Drucker philosophy the indispensable companion for their journeys. For the Leader to Leader Institute, it has never been enough to "keep his legacy alive." Instead, we strive to bring new energy, new resources, and new partnerships to our new challenges. Peter's light shines across the sectors, reaching leaders hungry for his messages that will illuminate, that will change their lives, and that in the end will move them to become more effective executives, the leaders of the future. That is the living legacy of Peter Drucker.

Before Peter died, I called him and reminded him of his statement to the Girl Scout board twenty years earlier: "We live in a country that pretends to care about its children, and it does not." I asked, "Peter, do you still feel the same way?" A long silence, then a sad voice. "Frances, has anything changed?"

He continued, "You and I know the answer. All we need to do is study the tragic statistics of children failing to get a high school diploma, the state of public education in the U.S., now ninth in the world. We used to be number one."

I often remind public, private, and social sector audiences that in the darkness of our times, Peter believed, "It is not business, it is not government, it is the social sector that may yet save the society." He was not a pessimist, but he was very sober about our times.

In 1954, when Peter had lived half his life, he wrote in *The Practice of Management* that "The purpose of the organization is to create a customer." And in the closing pages, "The business enterprise must be so managed as to make the public good become the private good of the enterprise." That was revolutionary in 1954; it is a powerful call to action today.

Peter's Qualities

I've had the privilege of sitting at the feet of Peter Drucker since 1981, participating in the founding of the Peter F. Drucker Foundation for Nonprofit Management, being one of those fortunate few who in 1990 and for the next twelve years could listen and learn from him as he attended all of the Drucker Foundation board meetings and all of our conferences; participated in and led video conferences; advised in the development of our tools, books, and videotapes; and wrote articles for our *Leader to Leader* journal. His philosophy permeated every aspect of our Drucker Foundation – Leader to Leader Institute initiatives, continues to do so, and always will.

It is difficult to think about Peter without remembering his gracious manners, his generosity, and the power of civility that were so much a part of who he was and how he did what he did. For those of us who knew him, he always provided a

"gift of example." He was enormously generous with his time
and his counsel. After that first transforming day with the Girl
Scouts, he gave us several days of his time for the next eight
years, just as he would pour his time, energy, and wisdom into
the Drucker Foundation for the following twelve years. We
learned about passion for the vision and the mission from Peter,
and thousands of our foundation members, authors, and participants shared that passion with a new kind of exuberance as
we worked to further his impact and his influence.

Peter Drucker had a rare gift, a genius unsurpassed:
he could develop a concept, a philosophy, and then distill
the language until the message was short, powerful, and
compelling. It is rare that a great mind, a great talent, a great
communicator can reach leaders at every level in every sector.
The power of the concept is too often diluted by paragraphs
and pages of explanation. Peter demonstrated the idea that
"communication is not saying something; communication
is being heard." Peter communicated in his short, powerful
messages. He told us, "Your mission should fit on a T-shirt."

Now, when I am attempting to define leadership in ways
that will connect with people, I often turn to Peter's wisdom,
tapping in to his genius for distilling the language into short,
inspiring messages that are powerful and relevant to our own
times and situations. Here are four of his observations that
help distill leadership to its essence:

1. The only definition of a leader is someone who has followers. Some people are thinkers. Some are prophets.
   Both roles are important and badly needed. But without
   followers, there can be no leaders.

2. An effective leader is not someone who is loved or admired. He or she is someone whose followers do the right things. Popularity is not leadership. Results are.
3. Leaders are highly visible. They therefore set examples.
4. Leadership is not rank, privileges, titles, or money. It is responsibility.

There are many of us who walk around remembering and trying to live Peter's expectations of us: "Think first. Speak last." We remember how at Drucker Foundation board meetings, he would sit quietly, listening to every word and then, at that magic moment, respond with the Drucker insight, in a few powerful sentences clarifying the issue, broadening the vision, and moving us into the future. Honoring the past but intensely defining the future was one of his great gifts.

For example, long, long ago he wrote that we would see the reunification of Germany, when no one else was making that statement. When the day came and the reunification had taken place, he was asked how he could have predicted this. His reply: "I never predict. I simply look out the window and see what is visible but not yet seen." In our tenuous times, when few attempt to predict the future, that one statement of Peter's philosophy encourages and inspires those who would be leaders of the future to look out the window, as Peter did, and see what is visible but not yet seen.

Each of us who knew Peter has his or her own stories. All of us are better for having our moments with this quiet, courteous giant who for a while walked among us, asking more questions than he offered answers, thinking first and speaking last, as he counseled us to do.

123

For me, one story stands out. In the days after September 11, when the staff and I were in our Drucker Foundation office in New York, I was concerned about how well we were carrying on, managing those tragic days and nights. So I called Peter and asked if he would send me a message that I could share with our staff and board. From Claremont came Peter's words:

September 18, 2001

To my Friends and Associates at the Drucker Foundation, New York City

Dear Friends:

Doris and I are most happy to learn from Frances that all of you are well and personally unscathed by this great tragedy. And I am sending all of you my most fervent wishes for a speedy and complete recovery from the emotional shock. Even out here — 3000 miles away — we haven't really recovered from it yet. And I am sure all of you realize that the mission and the work of the Drucker Foundation will only become more important in the months and years ahead. Till now the US had been the only major country free of terrorism — Germany, France, Japan went through several decades of it; the UK and Spain still live with it every day. If the experience of these countries teaches anything it is *not* to abandon daily life and civil society — that's exactly what the terrorist wants. It is, on the contrary, to *strengthen* daily life and civil society and to re-affirm their basic values and fundamental decencies. **And that is, after all, what the Drucker Foundation is all about.**

With affection and in warm friendship,

Peter F. Drucker
Claremont, California

When I learned of Peter's death on November 11, 2005, I was speaking at a conference in Tampa; I returned to New York and flew to California in time to attend the small, private memorial service at St. John's Episcopal Church, Monday afternoon, November 14, in LaVerne.

Doris Drucker, their four children and six grand-children, old friends, Claremont Graduate University representatives, Bob and Linda Buford, John Bachmann, and I were part of the group of twenty-five who gathered to celebrate his life. The Druckers' son Vincent, their daughter Cecily, and John Bachmann spoke, there was the liturgy, and the service ended with a quiet, moving moment as we all sang "Amazing Grace."

We have lost a quiet, powerful intellect, a warm and generous friend. Peter redefined the social sector, redefined society, redefined leadership and management—and gave mission, innovation, and values powerful new meanings that have changed our lives.

At the Leader to Leader Institute, formerly the Drucker Foundation, we continue to "live Peter Drucker," to move his message and his philosophy around the country and around the world. Every day, Peter's life and work are as relevant as they were the moment we became Drucker disciples long ago.

Peter Drucker's Interview with Frances Hesselbein at the Girl Scout Edith Macy Conference Center, September 1988

PETER F. DRUCKER (PFD): If you look back at these action-filled twelve years, what was your greatest accomplishment?

FRANCES HESSELBEIN (FH): I would say (1) managing for the mission and the wonderful sense of cohesion among our 335 councils and the national organization; (2) the broadest and deepest diversity the organization has ever known; and (3) the volunteer-staff partnership that liberates us to use our energies to further the mission without having battles over status.

PFD: What are the things that you have learned are most effective?

FH: We learned that we keep the mission before us. Every time a question arises, it's so easy to say, "If we do this, will it be good for girls? Will it be good for Girl Scouting? Will it further the mission? Will it help me do my work? Will it help other people?" If even one "no" emerges, then you don't do it.

PFD: You just said something very important. It's got to be right. If one "no" emerges, you don't do it. I think that's very, very important. *How* do you analyze this; how do you study this?

FH: We knew that once you have your mission in place, then you have to set goals. The board set the goals that were its vision of the desired future of the organization—this was the blueprint. Then the staff designed those objectives and action steps that would help us achieve the goals and further the mission. So Girl Scouting—every part of the organization—had a common planning management system—mission focused, values based. Once that was in place, the other "do" was looking at the mission and those goals, and asking *"How* do we deploy our people?" The delivery of services to Girl Scout councils always focused on girls, troops, and leaders. We tried to communicate in every possible way, always remembering—as you have said—that management, after all, is the management of people.

PFD: And now, some of the "don'ts." What have you learned especially that doesn't work in the Girl Scouts?

FH: The "Peanuts" character Charlie Brown has a wonderful quotation that I keep close to my heart. He says, "How can we lose when we are so sincere?" The answer is, it's easy. So we do not make assumptions about what other people think. Just because we are filled with "goodwill and human kindness," it doesn't mean that this is how we are perceived. We have learned that you don't do something at the national level and send it out to the troops. You bring council and national people together, and in teams develop the material and then field-test it. We learned that the more we include our constituents in the development of program resources, the more acceptable and the more successful they are.

PFD: You know, you said not one but at least three things. One, you said, don't be right, be conscientious. And the other thing is, don't try to convert all the people—test it and change it if need be. The third thing you said is, the people who have to use it have to be presold by being part of the development process so they know what they are trying to test and be convinced of it. These are very important things to say.

One thing you skipped over lightly is, where do these ideas, these challenges, come from?

FH: I think a "do not" would be, do not assume that all of the wisdom and all of the bright ideas are lodged in our management circles and groups and teams and the board. Never fail to listen to everyone's ideas—a troop leader in Boise, Idaho; a new committee member; the newest staff member; or a young man in the mail room. Everybody has something to bring: some of the brightest ideas and the best challenges come from the field or from an unexpected place. We have to be fluid, flexible, and appreciative enough to be open and welcome the ideas from wherever. To think that we have all the answers is fatal.

PFD: Now I am going to ask you about the things that didn't work. If you look back, what are the frustrations?

FH: How to manage time has been a frustration—how to find time for everything I need to do and want to do. I follow the principle that when doors open and there is a wonderful opportunity, you grab it. You can't say, come back in six months and talk to me. And so, daily and monthly I look at my calendar, and it is a source of embarrassment at best. It is hopelessly overscheduled, and, twelve years later, I don't do any better with managing my own time. But honestly, Peter, I truly have not experienced great frustration. I think frustration comes when you want to do something and there are so many barriers in the way. I have had great freedom and scope.

PFD: And now, look ahead a little bit.

FH: I see the great challenge to our organization—it goes far beyond us, of course—is to really understand the challenge of the demographics, to see the rapidly changing demographics as enormous opportunity for us to serve in new and more significant ways than ever before—not to see this as a threat. We need to anticipate the kinds of program supports we will need and have them ready as these trends emerge. It's being astute enough to catch a straw in the wind even before it's a trend, and then have everything in place when it emerges and not run to catch up; to understand the character of the organization and the importance of seeing these opportunities, not in terms of numbers and money, but in terms of service and the potential of each girl.

And, in our eagerness to find the children of the Hmong, or the children of Vietnamese immigrants, or Mexican Americans, we must not forget that the little girl in the suburbs in the basement of the Second Presbyterian Church also deserves equal access. There's something dramatic about serving the children of the Hmong, but we cannot forget that the children in West Virginia also have enormous needs. So equal access must mean equal access.

I would hope in six, in eight, and in ten years, we would be celebrating the remarkable diversity of a strong pluralistic organization in a pluralistic society. We would be one of the great cohesion builders in communities that are losing their cohesion. I would see us serving girls in new and more significant ways through this solid determination to provide equal access. As communities deteriorate further, we would be a powerful force to help build the cohesion or hold it in communities.

Another area would be for our 738,000 adult members—which makes us one of the largest adult education institutions in the country—we would provide the most remarkable continuing adult education opportunities of any institution in the country.

I think those are two ways we could play a significant and stronger role than ever before. The third would be GSUSA as a powerful voice on issues that affect girls and the mission. And that is it—not dissipating our energies, but keep focusing on why we are an organization—on the mission.

PFD: And this is really what you laid the foundation for, all of you, these last twelve years.

FH: We didn't know it; we thought we were just doing our work. But I think you are right. We really laid the foundation for the future because we tried to think of the future as we made decisions and of what impact those decisions would have.

PFD: Frances, when you leave the Girl Scout organization and they hang your portrait on the wall, there will be a little brass plaque below the frame. What will be the inscription on that plaque?

FH: I hope it says, "She never broke a promise."

PFD: No. It will say, "She kept the faith."

CHAPTER 10

THE INDISPENSABLE PARTNERSHIP— GOVERNANCE AND MANAGEMENT, BOARD AND STAFF

Our times are teaching us a lesson about the indispensability of effective governance and management in all three sectors—public, private, and social. Over the past several years, headlines and nightly newscasts have delivered tragic stories of failed leaders—chairmen, presidents, CEOs—unfaithful to mission, oblivious to fiduciary responsibility, disrespectful of the workforce, and disdainful of the stockholders' and the public interest.

After the shock and disbelief that we feel with each disclosure—and the list of failed and failing corporations, organizations, and public agencies grows longer—all of us who serve on boards or lead the management of an organization ask, "What is our company, our enterprise doing today to prevent the betrayal of trust tomorrow?" We may think only of headlined corporate scandals, yet this crisis crosses all three sectors. Social sector organizations and the institutions of government carry their share of this burden.

We have seen the CEO who withholds information from the board of governors, tries to manipulate the board, or selects cronies from the "good old boy" network who are nothing more than window dressing. And sometimes the board insists on second-guessing the CEO or tries to go around the CEO to issue instructions to members of the management team. Whatever the immediate cause, the board – CEO relationship is dysfunctional. They work at cross-purposes or see each other as adversaries, rather than as partners leading the organization.

The Power of Partnership

When I was the national executive director (CEO) of the Girl Scouts of the USA, I had the privilege of serving with our three successive presidents (the Girl Scouts use the title of president for the officer who chairs the board of directors) in amazingly successful partnerships. We had remarkable volunteers who chaired and served on the board, and the majority of them understood the power of the partnership with management. The staff would do its work, and we would bring clear proposals to the board for its consideration. It was a powerful, positive partnership. I was responsible for a total staff of more than eight hundred national staff members and six thousand local council staff members in the beginning.

By the time I left thirteen years later, I had worked with three national board chairmen—Dr. Gloria Scott, Jane

Freeman, and, in my final term, Betty Pilsbury. They were all unique personalities and remarkable leaders. We observed a clear and sharp differentiation of governance and management: the board was responsible for vision, mission, and goals; management was responsible for taking those and responding with clear objectives and action steps for management that would further the mission and achieve the goals. The board never tried to get involved with management issues, nor the staff in governance matters. If you're not all together, if you are wasting your time on turf battles and on trying to determine roles, if there is lack of respect on either side for the positions of the chairman and the CEO—you lose ground. You are wasting time that you should be spending leading the organization. Mutual respect and appreciation was our message.

The Philosophy of No Surprises

For thirteen years our partnership worked with highly visible success. Some obvious reasons for that success were the common commitment to mission (our reason for being); visibly living the values; respecting the clear and sharp differentiation of governance and management; a shared vision of a desired future where Girl Scouting would take the lead in our society in helping each girl reach her own highest potential; and building the diverse, inclusive, effective organization of the future. Our circular management system, "managing in a world that is round," brought down the old hierarchical walls, so that teamwork could move *across* the organization. The list is long, but there is one that we talked about, practiced, and shared widely. It was "the philosophy of no surprises," as important in personal relationships, the family, and the workplace as it is for leaders in all three sectors.

Betty Pilsbury, the last president I worked with as national executive director, shared my passion for this philosophy. When we would go to our Edith Macy Conference Center to talk with new council presidents or new council executive directors, we would sit on two tall stools for our leadership dialogue.

We would talk about the privilege of serving as the national leadership team of this largest organization for girls and young women in the world, about how the ways of working together we all had developed were highly productive, with measureable results; about how we balanced various demands; about how we worked to focus on those few areas that would make the greatest difference. The joy of our shared task and partnership was apparent.

At some point the exchange would go something like this: Betty would say to me, "Frances, have I ever done anything or said anything at a board meeting that surprised you?" I would say, "No, never." Then I would ask, "Betty, have I ever done anything, said anything at a board meeting that surprised you?" Her reply, "Never." Then together we would smile and say, together in unison, "The philosophy of no surprises!"

To this day, I try to be faithful to this philosophy. Nothing builds or sustains trust more effectively. Nothing strengthens the team approach to management and builds inclusion and respect more than sharing the message. Then we are all on the communications sled together.

"Do I have a surprise for you!"—neatly packaged and delivered, with no involvement, engagement, or inclusion of our people—is part of the leadership of the past. As Peter Drucker reminded us, "The leader of the past tells. The leader of the future asks. Ask, don't tell."

When Betty and I were developing our "no surprises" philosophy, we were not aware of Drucker's "Ask, don't tell" expression. If we had been, we would have embraced his powerful language, just as our philosophy and performance embraced his concept before we knew about it. We found that "What do you think about this?" is far more effective than "Now, hear this" for both governance and management.

Because the board and staff together worked so effectively at the national and council levels, we were able to accomplish what many called "the transformation of the Girl Scouts of the USA." Openness, trust, and shared vision, mission, and values were essential ingredients to building One Great Movement. Inclusion and respect were basic to the philosophy of no surprises.

As I recounted earlier, Peter Drucker told me after his first visit to our New York headquarters, "I can tell a lot about an organization from its building. In this building the culture is palpable." If we define culture as "the beliefs and values practiced by an organization," then the beliefs and values were communicated in every action, the practices were documented, and the organization flourished. "No surprises" was an essential ingredient.

Critical Questions

We are learning bitter lessons from the failures of flawed leaders and indifferent boards. The litany is long—of board members who are unaware or indifferent to dubious financial practices; who are ignorant of salaries, benefits, and loans; and who do not ask the critical questions or request the clarification or additional information required for informed decisions. In these times, wise leaders in all three sectors no longer blithely agree to serve on a board without asking serious questions. A few years ago, this might not have been the case; today such questioning is essential.

In serving as chairman of the Volunteers of America for six years; as chairman and founding president of the Drucker Foundation (now the Leader to Leader Institute) for ten years; as the CEO of Girl Scouts of the USA for thirteen years; and as a member of the boards of Mutual of America Life Insurance Company, Pennsylvania Power and Light, and other organizations, I have learned that there are serious questions every potential director should ask before accepting an invitation to join a board:

- **What is the mission of the organization?** The response should tell you why they do what they do—the organization's reason for being. If there is no mission statement or if the response focuses on the *what* ("Let me tell you what we do") and not the *why* they do what they do, say good-bye.
- **What is the board's vision of the future?** This question should bring an illuminating response. No vision—you don't sign on. Some visions of the future are so compelling that you accept *almost* before you go down the list of

questions a prudent potential board members asks. Others make it simple to decline.

- **Is there a positive partnership of the chairman and the president or CEO?** The board should see the president as a partner of the board, not a subordinate. A positive partnership here provides a model for the board, the staff, and the enterprise.
- **Does the president or CEO appreciate and observe the clear and sharp differentiation between governance and management?** The demarcation between governance and management is critical, with management not attempting to establish policy and the board not attempting to manage the organization.
- **Is this a learning organization?** Look for continuing leadership learning opportunities for both board and staff.
- **Are the corporation's most recent audit, yearly financial report, and annual report delivered along with the invitation to serve?** If not provided, politely decline.
- **What is the climate at board meetings?** Check to see if there are comprehensive background material, energetic engagement, and full disclosure before the board decides on an action.
- **Does the board, as Peter Drucker advises, see the president as "the hinge to the board"?** Other members of the management team should not have personal relationships with board members, creating power pockets that can diminish and divide.
- **Does the organization provide Directors and Officers insurance?** If the answer is no, you cannot accept the invitation to serve.

- **What does the organization hope I will contribute as a new board member?** Ask yourself as well what you will bring to this board that will help the organization further the mission, achieve the goals, and build the organization of the future.

Planning, Policy, and Review

Beyond the listed questions, a clear understanding and commitment to planning, policy, and review (PPR)—the three major, generic areas of board responsibility for all enterprises—are essential:

Planning. The board has the responsibility for strategic planning, establishing mission and goals, and reviewing
these every two or three years against an environmental
scan that helps the board identify major emerging trends
and their implications for the future of the organization.

Policy. The board determines all policies that the organization must adhere to. Policies on salaries, benefits,
and other compensation, as well as policies involving partnerships, alliances, and collaboration—all need
to ensure that objectives and action steps presented
by management will achieve the goals and further the
mission of the organization.

Review (oversight). This third critical responsibility demands
careful study, understanding, and approval of all management actions and reports, including acceptance of
the audit and financial reports; approval of change in
direction, consistent with mission and goals; and the

annual performance appraisal of the president or CEO, with a review of the previous year and acceptance of the president's goals for the new year.

The PPR approach, carried out in good faith by board members who took their governance responsibilities seriously, would have prevented the sad ending of careers and the failures of many companies and organizations. The awareness that board members are the custodians of public trust and money and bear a tough fiduciary responsibility is a necessary background to the exciting dialogue we engage in when we are asked to serve on a board of directors, knowing it could be a great adventure in civic responsibility.

Exemplary Board – CEO Partnerships

Fortunately, beyond the headlines of the moment lie thousands of powerful partnerships of the chairman and the president, the board and management, that meet and exceed the ethical, responsible standards and expectations of public trust, public money, and public support. Let me share two experiences.

Several years ago, I chaired the national board of directors of Volunteers of America, one of our oldest human service organizations (then 107 years old), with "there are no limits to caring" as a reminder of who we were. Before the board went into session, the board and management team often spent a half day examining critical issues as background for planning and review. We did this periodically to ensure that we were aware of emerging trends and issues that would have the greatest impact on our work and on those we serve.

The president, Chuck Gould, and I tried to model the essential partnership that must be effective if we are going to be viable, relevant, and faithful to our mission in the future — just as the total board, the management team, and those in the field must see themselves as effective partners. For us, the philosophy of no surprises was a powerful concept for a chairman – president partnership that was open, stimulating, and productive, with total trust and mutual appreciation.

I also serve on the board of Mutual of America Life Insurance Company, where the partnership of its chairman, president, and CEO, Tom Moran, with his management team is as powerful as the partnership of its board and management. Mutual of America's management is a model of openness, energetic engagement of a distinguished board, total transparency, and an inspiring vision of the future of the organization and of the society.

I carry lessons learned from these great organizations wherever I go — derived not from the theory of governance and management, but from shared experience, deep involvement, and critical observation. These and other examples balance, for me, the tragic stories of companies and organizations that betrayed the public trust and failed themselves and their workers, shareholders, and stakeholders. For all over this country are hundreds of thousands of corporations and social sector organizations that strive and succeed in building the quality of governance, management, and results that our institutions and the public they serve require and deserve.

CHAPTER 11

STRENGTHENING THE LEADERSHIP OF THE SOCIAL SECTOR

The economic, social, and environmental challenges we face in this new century are enormous. Although the social sector can lead the way, no single sector alone can address these challenges, which are both local and global in scope. The public, private, and nonprofit sectors must be equally vibrant if we are to build healthy societies. Leaders from all three sectors must work and lead beyond the walls of their own enterprises to achieve significant results. Helping meet this challenge would become the next exciting phase of my journey.

On January 31, 1990, I said good-bye to the Girl Scouts of the USA, the best organization, the best people in the world. It was a perfect time to leave. We had reached the highest membership, the greatest diversity, and the greatest cohesion in our seventy-eight-year history. We were one great movement, mission focused, values based, and demographics driven. We had listened to our customers, some of them only five years old. That last year, a carefully planned twelve months of leadership transition, was the most exuberant year of my career.

I presented all 335 council executive directors with a small pewter box; on the lid, there was an engraving of the Girl Scout logo, the date, and a message: "Thank you for keeping the faith. Frances Hesselbein." I keep mine on my desk in New York, a reminder of an incredible journey with incredible men and women who embodied the mission in all they were and did, and who "kept the faith" with girls, parents, the community, and the society.

Establishing the Peter F. Drucker Foundation for Nonprofit Management

The morning after I left the Girls Scouts, I received a call from the then chairman of Mutual of America, William Flynn: "Frances, when are you coming to see your office?"

Taken aback, I said, "Bill, I don't have an office; I just left my office."

"You aren't listening," Bill said. "When are you coming to see your office?"

So I went over to the Mutual of America headquarters, then at 666 Fifth Avenue. Bill ushered me up to the nineteenth floor and showed me an impressive executive office with my name on the door. He said, "This company does not know what you are going to do in the future, but whatever you do will help our clients. So you have to have an office. Here it is, and out there is a half secretary." I was grateful and overwhelmed.

In mid-March, six weeks later, Bob Buford, the head of Buford Television in Texas; Dick Schubert, president of the Points of Light Foundation and former president of the American Red Cross; and I (all of us enormously influenced by Peter Drucker in our careers) flew to Claremont to brainstorm about how we could spread and apply Peter's works and philosophy to the nonprofit sector. That afternoon and evening, we worked for hours, covering the room with newsprint. What we came up with was the Peter F. Drucker Foundation for Nonprofit Management, a foundation that would deal not in money but in intellectual capital and that would spread the Drucker philosophy across the nonprofit world. We would invite Peter to have breakfast with us the next morning at Griswald's Inn and present our brainchild to our friend, our inspiration—the father of modern management.

Peter arrived for breakfast, suspicious, giving us a look: *What are these three characters up to?* Bob, Dick, and I took turns, dancing around the room with our newsprint, presenting our case. We couldn't tell what Peter was thinking. Finally, at the end of our presentation, he looked up and said, "We will not name it for me. I am not dead yet, and I don't intend to become an icon." (It was the only battle he lost.) "We will not focus on me. There are a lot of good people out there, and you will bring them all in." Already he had expanded our vision.

Bob said that he and Dick had decided that I should be chairman of the new board. After all, I had just left the Girl Scouts and would have time for several board meetings a year. (I had bought a place in Pennsylvania, promised a publisher I would write a book on leadership, and was not going to travel so much.)

Peter looked at me and said, "You will not be the chairman. You will be the president and CEO and run it, or it won't work." Who could refuse Peter Drucker, our new honorary chairman?

I flew back to New York, went to Mutual of America, and said, "We have just established the Peter F. Drucker Foundation for Nonprofit Management. Do you mind if it moves in on top of me?" The chairman's response was immediate: "No, and when you need more room, it will be available."

So six weeks after leaving the world's largest organization for girls and women, I was now the CEO of probably the smallest foundation in the world. We had no money or staff, but we did have an office (the gift of Mutual of America), a passionate vision and mission, and Peter on board to inspire, question, challenge, and work hand in hand with a new board and staff. From March to September we worked to build that board and a small staff, organizing to launch the new foundation.

In October 1990, Peter Drucker spoke at the annual conference of The Independent Sector (a national association of nonprofit organizations founded by John W. Gardner), and later that day Peter and I talked with reporters in a press conference to announce the official birth of the Peter F. Drucker Foundation for Nonprofit Management. One of the reporters asked Peter what the first initiative of the new Drucker Foundation would be. The father of modern management replied, "An organizational self-assessment tool."

We had never discussed this, yet he turned to me and asked, "Frances, how long will it take? Two years?" I responded blithely, "Oh no—eighteen months should be enough."

In 1990, the greatest need in the nonprofit sector was a self-assessment tool that an organization's board and staff could use, that a management team could use in revisiting the mission, conducting a performance appraisal of the organization's results, and developing a strategic plan. We knew that the organization of the future had to be able to assess past and present performance to chart a viable path ahead. For an organization to assess its own performance honestly and rigorously takes courage. Peter was issuing a call to action to nonprofit leaders everywhere to have the courage to lead. I discuss the Self-Assessment Tool in more detail in a later section.

Felicitous is one way to describe our journey with Peter. Every day we spent together on books, conferences, dialogues, or videos was a day never to be forgotten, always to be cherished. However, there was one small cloud in the sky over the new Drucker Foundation. As I mentioned earlier, when Bob Buford, Dick Schubert, and I founded it, Peter declared I had to be the president and CEO—not the chairman, as we had planned. I looked at the great gifts the new foundation was receiving: our beautiful offices, courtesy of Mutual of America; some of our country's greatest corporate and nonprofit leaders offering to serve on that first board; and great thought leaders eager to write for us and speak for us, all as their own contribution to Peter Drucker's foundation, never accepting an honorarium for speaking or articles. I decided that in consideration of this enormous outpouring of generous support, as well as of Peter's time and devotion to the new enterprise, I would serve as president and CEO, but I could not accept the CEO salary; I would live on my Girl Scout retirement. The salary and all my speaking honoraria would be my personal contribution to the Drucker Foundation.

This was a great issue with Peter. At every board meeting, he would say, "You have to take the salary. You must take the salary." My response: "I'm sorry, but this is the only way I will serve as president and CEO." Finally, one day at a board meeting, Peter said, "It is immoral and obscene that you do not take the salary." I replied, "All right, Peter, I'm going to tell people you called me 'immoral and obscene.'" Peter looked at the board members and said, "What can you do with this woman?" End of argument, end of story. It was our only disagreement in over twenty years of enormously inspiring work together. It was the right battle to be fought, and I had to win. For the ten years I was the CEO, I never took the salary, and for twenty years, all my speaking honoraria have gone directly to the Drucker Foundation, now the Leader to Leader Institute.

A Magnet for Talent

Early on in the new foundation's life, with only two staff members doing incredible work, a man came to see me, a recently retired executive with Metropolitan Life Insurance Company. Clarence Pearson introduced himself and said, "John Creedon says you could use some help, and he said I should volunteer." (As I have recounted, while president of MetLife, John Creedon led a Girl Scout campaign that raised $10 million to build the new Edith Macy Conference Center.) Here was a former executive of MetLife eager to join our staff. The next day, Clarence became our new vice president. So we had a pro bono president and vice president, along with offices that were a gift.

More volunteers arrived, eager to bring Peter's work and philosophy to the social sector. From the first moment of the Drucker Foundation's existence until today at the Leader to Leader Institute, we have had the same lawyer, Ken Kirschner, whose legal services are a gift. From 1990 until now, he has served us as his contribution, although he does not like me to mention it.

Generous hearts, generous spirits like these have moved a small foundation to its position today. Other longtime friends and advisers, such as Dr. John W. Work III, Murray Dropkin, and Marshall Goldsmith, contributed their time and expertise generously.

We all shared a dream. Peter was our leader. Hundreds, thousands of friends all over the world joined us in their own way, in their own time, until, today as I write this chapter, we have just celebrated Peter's one hundredth birthday and are now celebrating the twentieth anniversary of the Drucker Foundation – Leader to Leader Institute.

And it all began with gifts of time, gifts of space, and gifts of thoughts—spoken and written—gifts, each offered in the giver's own way, to move Peter's inspiration, his philosophy, and his wisdom around the country and around the world. By now, more than four hundred great thought leaders have written and spoken for us. Best of all, this generous outpouring continues to this day: twenty years of giving, not to an individual, but to Peter's vision, the board and staff's vision, the vision of strengthening the social sector.

Of all the generous gifts to the foundation, Peter's heart and mind and caring were the greatest gifts of all. He taught us, "It's not about us; it's about them."

Twenty years after its beginning, the Drucker Foundation – Leader to Leader Institute continues to be the guest of Mutual of America. When we grew, the office space was there. Two generations of Mutual of America's officers— twenty years of generous, indispensable support—add up to a powerful example of corporate social responsibility. It's a long way from "When are you coming to see your office?" to our twenty-sixth book, *The Organization of the Future 2*. I am deeply grateful to this great American corporation, our fellow traveler on the journey to significance. Recently, when I went to the U.S. Military Academy at West Point for my first "leadership dialogue" (I am serving as the Class of 1951 Chair for the Study of Leadership, a two-year appointment), Tom Moran, the chairman, president, and CEO of Mutual of America, was the first great leader to join me in dialogue. The cadets loved him.

Challenges and Accomplishments

The Drucker Foundation began with a simple challenge: How do we share the best thinking on leadership and management with the leaders of social sector organizations? Our mission was "to lead social sector organizations toward excellence in performance." We later refined this to be "to strengthen the leadership of the social sector." Although at first some thought we would be addressing only the leaders of U.S. organizations, it soon became clear that the issues of managing for the mission and building a more responsive, inclusive institution had worldwide relevance and appeal. For example, in 1992, we partnered with the W. K. Kellogg Foundation to present the Salzburg Seminar on Managing Nongovernmental Organizations for fifty-four Fellows from thirty-four nations. The Leader to Leader Institute continues to broaden its scope to reach beyond the walls of geography, culture, and sector.

In 1993, we took a significant step toward moving Peter's works and wisdom around the world with the publication of *The Five Most Important Questions You Will Ever Ask About Your Nonprofit Organization: The Drucker Foundation Self-Assessment Tool*, the project Peter surprised me with at our press conference. The Self-Assessment Tool presents the five most important questions for any organization to ask:

1. What is our mission?
2. Who is our customer?
3. What does the customer value?
4. What are our results?
5. What is our plan?

When the questions are the right questions, they move beyond the social sector and are equally relevant for business and government—and they are global. Use of the Self-Assessment Tool spread quickly, extending far beyond the

United States. In Argentina, for example, Compromiso, a community foundation in Buenos Aires, received a large grant from Coca-Cola to conduct an organizational self-assessment of the country's public schools using the five questions. One of the participants in Compromiso's Schools for Change program reported, "The program didn't give us money or goods, as we hoped it would in the beginning. But it gave us something much more precious: the know-how to get the money and the goods for ourselves."

You may be sure that when we first developed the Drucker Foundation Self-Assessment Tool, we were not thinking of the public schools of Argentina or of government agencies but of nonprofit organizations in our own country. Compromiso has published a Spanish version of the Self-Assessment Tool for its own use and has made it available throughout Latin America. Today, leaders all over the world are using the third edition of the Self-Assessment Tool, now titled *Peter Drucker's Five Most Important Questions*.

As honorary chairman of our foundation, Peter wrote the lead article for the first issue of our new journal, *Leader to Leader*, in 1993, which also carried articles by Jim Collins, John W. Gardner, Steve Kerr, and Rosabeth Moss Kanter. The title of Peter's article was "The Shape of Things to Come." Like almost everything he ever wrote, it is as relevant and powerful now as the day he wrote it. That year also marked the publication of our first book, *The Leader of the Future*, which Marshall Goldsmith, Richard Beckhard, and I edited. It was a best seller, and was quickly followed by *The Organization of the Future* and *The Community of the Future*.

All found a wide and responsive audience. Many more books followed over the years.

We were recognized in the *New York Times* on the front page of the business section with the headline "Thinking Great Thoughts Without Great Money," with a photograph of Peter and me. The January 12, 2000, article by Fred Andrews stated, "Dwight MacDonald, the acerbic essayist, once described the Ford Foundation as a large body of money surrounded by people who want some. The Peter F. Drucker Foundation for Nonprofit Management, with little money, is a pool of management wisdom for all who choose to dip their cup."

For twenty years, Peter's expectation that we "would bring them all in" has been proven valid. There are now more than four hundred great thought leaders who have either written for us, spoken for us, or traveled with us abroad. We have twenty-six books in thirty languages. When our newest book, *The Leader of the Future 2*, was published recently, the first four countries to buy the publishing rights to the book were South Korea, Vietnam, Indonesia, and China. And it all began that March day in a small room in Griswald's Inn, Claremont, California, with Peter Drucker's expansion of our dream—guiding us beyond the walls, across the country and around the world—led by the power of his life and his message. I quote Peter Drucker in every speech I make, and I speak twice a week in this country to leaders in all three sectors, and three times a year abroad. Always his words are a memorable part of the speech.

When Peter's health was failing, we thought the most respectful thing to do was return the name to his family, and with his blessing we took our *Leader to Leader* journal's name and became the Leader to Leader Institute, with the same mission and a vision of helping spread the news of Peter Drucker's inspired life, work, and philosophy around the country and around the world. Shortly after the transition, Peter wrote, "I am delighted that the Leader to Leader Institute is now successfully underway. When we started the original Drucker Foundation 12 years ago, our intent was to create an advisor to the social sector in leadership, management, innovation and other key areas. Many of our goals have been achieved, and now it's time to move forward with the new Institute."

Like the social sector organizations we serve, the Leader to Leader Institute relies on volunteers to help us further our mission. We are singularly fortunate in having many generous partners, colleagues, and friends who help us make a difference in the social sector. Today Peter's spirit lives on, and our Leader to Leader Institute and all those whose lives we touch will continue to shine Peter's light.

CHAPTER 12

ADVENTURES AROUND THE WORLD

The Navy had a slogan, "Join the Navy and see the world!" I never joined the Navy, but the Girl Scouts did provide my first opportunity to see the world. As I have recounted, my first trip abroad was to Greece in the 1960s when I was serving in a volunteer role on the national board of directors (long before I ever became the CEO); I was one of six representatives of GSUSA at the triennial World Conference of Girl Guides and Girl Scouts.

While on the national board I also had the opportunity to serve as one of two American women on the Our Chalet committee of the World Association of Girl Guides and Girl Scouts, meeting every February and September in Adelboden, Switzerland. Our Chalet was an inspiring world center, a magnificent traditional Swiss chalet in the Alps, built by a Boston woman, Blanche Storrow, as a place where girls and young women from all over the world could come together in peace and understanding. Storrow is remembered for her philanthropy in Boston; she is remembered by generations of Girl Scouts worldwide for making possible this beautiful conference center high in the Alps, where they come in friendship and love, and leave with a learning experience that stays with them forever. Girls from over two hundred countries have made Our Chalet their own.

Whether with the Girl Scouts, the Drucker Foundation, or the Leader to Leader Institute, I've had the privilege to speak or to represent the United States in sixty-eight countries, including England, Greece, Kenya, South Africa, Iran, the Philippines, South Korea, China, Australia, and New Zealand. Every experience strengthens my belief in the power of common values, common vision, and common language (translated wherever needed). When we share a vision of healthy children, strong families, good schools, safe neighborhoods, decent housing, work that dignifies—all embraced by the healthy, diverse, inclusive community that cares about all of its children, all of its people, the minor issues that divide us fade away, and we all move together toward that bright future that shimmers in the distance.

There is an amazing openness I find in these meetings today—whether with the Chevron-Texaco Management Institute, the National Urban League, the Eisenhower Conference on National Security, Goodwill Industries, Bright China, the Royal Plunket Society of New Zealand, American university presidents and their teams, the Salzburg Seminar in Austria, or Greek and Turkish Cypriot teenagers. I value my moments with these people—all different in age, tradition, discipline, sector, history, and experience—yet all reflecting the challenges of our time and the future yet to be revealed, and all committed to moving to a new level of leadership and service.

Our times are sobering for thoughtful leaders. Transformation, cultural change, discontinuity, chaos, values, entrepreneurship, strategic thinking, and leadership imperatives animate questions and discussions. Across all sectors, leaders are searching for ways to respond to the most volatile, rapidly changing times anyone can remember. They know they face tough questions and that there are more to come.

Some recent questions frame the dialogue across the sectors: How can we challenge the gospel—doing things the way we've always done them? How do we meet greater needs with diminishing resources? How do we bridge the divide between the field and the national organization? Is it possible to have dispersed leadership in a traditional hierarchical company? How do we provide equal access in today's climate? In these turbulent times, the questions we ask are almost more significant than the responses.

Let me share two stories from my recent travels.

Love, Faith, and Peace to Us All

When was the last time you flew over giant snow-covered mountain peaks and then landed near palm trees and a beautiful beach? I had this experience not long ago, traveling from New York through San Francisco to Auckland, and finally to Dunedin on New Zealand's South Island.

A great number of friends and colleagues had wanted to come along with me to New Zealand "to carry my bags." It isn't just because *Lord of the Rings* was filmed there. Here at home there is enormous interest in a small country with "four million people and sixty-four million sheep" that protects its environment. "You can drink from the aquifer," as everyone told me, and the air is pure; the environment is everyone's responsibility, and in its respect and inclusion of its native people, the country is an inspiring model for us all.

The magnificence of the island was exceeded only by the welcome of the people of New Zealand and the sig- nificance of the meetings—ten days never to be forgotten. I was in the country to be honored as the first woman and the fifteenth American leader to receive the Fulbright New Zealand John F. Kennedy Memorial Fellowship. When Pres- ident Kennedy was assassinated, New Zealand established the John F. Kennedy Memorial Fellowship in his honor. It is administered by Fulbright New Zealand and presented at the American embassy. Every few years, an American leader is chosen as the John F. Kennedy Fellow and brought to New Zealand to speak on leadership and voluntarism to a number of groups across the country.

In my first major speech, "Leaders of the Future— Leadership Imperatives," I addressed the Royal Plunket Society's hundredth anniversary celebration in Dunedin, with fifteen hundred people in the audience. For one hundred years the nurses of the New Zealand Royal Plunket Society have called on every new mother and her baby—"a healthy start for every baby." Today they are reaching 92 percent of all newborn babies born in New Zealand. Can you imagine the difference all over the world if every newborn baby and its mother had a visit from a nurse, making sure the mother and baby had the care and materials they needed? (On my flight to New Zealand, a flight attendant asked me why I was visiting, and when I said my first speech would be in Dunedin to the Royal Plunket Society, every flight attendant said proudly, "I am a Plunket baby.")

Before I spoke, two Maori leaders opened the session in a very moving way, calling on the spirits to bless the gathering. In fact, Maori leaders were at every gathering, opening every meeting, an integral part of each event—an inspiring example of what can happen in a country when all cultures and all people are recognized, respected, and involved. New Zealand and the Maori have become a positive case study for our daily efforts in building bridges, in involving all of our people, in building that healthy, diverse, inclusive society that cares about all of its people. Parts of the trip were almost a spiritual experience, and I was moved and deeply impressed by the positive inclusion of the Maori and other peoples in the life of the country.

In this speech as well as in others around the country (for I spoke several times a day), I always found a place to share President Kennedy's message in his inaugural address: "And so, my fellow Americans, ask not what your country can do for you, ask what you can do for your country." We often forget the second part of this message: "And my fellow citizens of the world: Ask not what America will do for you, but what together we can do for the freedom of Man." At the Royal Plunket Society, I stressed (as I always do) the need to build a diverse, inclusive, cohesive organization, with rich representation at every level, if we are to be viable and relevant—or even present—five or ten years from now.

I am passionate in my expression of this leadership imperative, and something in my message touched five Maori

157

women who were present as the Maori caucus of the Plunket board. The big audience of several thousand was wonderfully responsive, and as the applause ended and people started filing out, I walked down from the stage, where one of my escorts, Lynn, was waiting. She said, "The Maori women would like to meet with you." I walked over to where the five Maori women were standing in a half circle. Nothing prepared me for the ceremony that followed, but instinctively I knew what to do. The first woman took my hands in hers and lightly touched her nose to mine; we looked into each other's eyes and held that position until the spirit within had connected. (This is my interpretation.) Then I moved to the next Maori leader and clasped her hands; we pressed our noses together, and our eyes communicated. This continued until all five women had greeted me, made me part of the circle. Then the six of us clasped hands, and in a circle, they sang a beloved Maori song, "Te Aroha, Te Whakapono, Me Te Rangimarie" ("Love, Faith, and Peace to Us All"), in three-part harmony.

Some of the audience heard that a rare and sacred Maori ceremony was taking place, and they came back and stood quietly in the rear; when the Maori women sang the first verse of "Love," they all joined in the chorus and sang it back to us in the Maori language. Then the Maori women hung a cord around my neck with a sacred green stone (called *pounamu*—jade). It was one-half dark green, one-half lighter green. One woman pointed to the lighter half and said, "This is you," and then to the darker half, saying "This is us." Jade is considered a treasure by Maoris. This ceremony has deep meaning, not just for me, but for all those who observed this rare and beautiful moment bringing us all together. I will always remember it.

After I told this story to the students attending the University of Pittsburgh Hesselbein Global Academy Summit at our inaugural summit in 2009, a young university student from Hawaii came forward, and as she hung a black wooden bead lei around my neck, she said with great emotion, "My mother is Maori." There were many tears. I was moved by how many of our summit students, in their notes to me afterwards, ended with the words "Love, Faith, and Peace to Us All."

The Ocean of the Future

I have the privilege of serving on the board of the Graduate School of International Relations and Pacific Studies at the University of California, San Diego, and while I was there I discovered a profound message hanging on the wall of our meeting room. In 1898, the Honorable John Jay, Secretary of State, wrote, "The Mediterranean is the ocean of the past. The Atlantic is the ocean of the present. The Pacific is the ocean of the future." That was over one hundred years ago. John Jay's prescience was extraordinary.

I also have the honor of serving as one of three Americans on the board of directors of Bright China Social Fund, a new foundation created by the great Chinese philanthropist, business entrepreneur, and educator Shao Ming Lo. He is founder and chairman of Bright China Holding Ltd., the Peter F. Drucker Academy, and the Bright China Foundation in China. The Bright China Foundation has made donations to build and operate schools in the northwest and southwest of China, providing educational opportunities to more than three thousand students from poverty-stricken farming families. In 1999, Shao founded Bright China Management Institute. He studied under the tutorship of Peter Drucker at Claremont, hoping to make available to China's executives and entrepreneurs the best of the world's management thought.

I made my first trip to China in 2000 as the guest of Shao Ming Lo. When I was planning the trip to speak in Beijing and Shenzhen, I suggested to Chairman Shao that instead of coming alone, I would bring a team of three remarkable leaders who would pay their own travel expenses just for the privilege of being part of this significant opportunity. Shao was delighted to accept the team, so I was accompanied by three remarkable people: Kenneth Kirschner, one of the five best lawyers in his field in the United States; Richard Ciecka, also a lawyer, a student of Eastern culture, and then president of Capital Management, the investment arm of Mutual of America; and Iain Somerville, then a global affairs and strategy consultant with Accenture. All three took care of their own travel as their contribution, took a week from their busy schedules, and connected in a powerful way in Beijing, Shenzhen, and Dongguan with every audience.

I felt wonderful as the plane landed in Beijing early in the morning. The Bright China people met us with a warm welcome and said that there were so many people who wanted us to speak while we were in China that the plan for us to rest on the day we landed had been changed. This was the only day for sightseeing. Would we like to visit the university or the Great Wall of China? We chose the Great Wall, and off we went to the most inspiring beginning of an incredible adventure in learning. I love the photographs of that day, as we climbed the Great Wall.

I had had both hips replaced several months before the trip, and when I told Chairman Shao that I had had this surgery, he was concerned, but I assured him that the hips were working perfectly, better than new. The first three days in Beijing, I had two wonderful aides—Lynn and a gentleman who spoke little English. He insisted on carrying my briefcase; Lynn carried my handbag. Because the gentleman was with us every moment, I asked Lynn about him. "Oh, he works in a hospital," she said vaguely. Wherever we went—for three speeches a day, interviews, dialogue-packed days—they were at my side. I had never had such solicitous care for three whole days; they appeared at breakfast and took me back to the hotel at night.

On my last day in Beijing, as I was saying good-bye and thank you to my two companions, the gentleman said in careful English, "I hear you speak. You great woman leader. This is for you." And he handed me a CD, *Music of Ancient China*. Later, I asked Lynn once again, "Who is this kind man?" This time she responded, "He is China's greatest surgeon. Chairman Shao wanted him to be with you these three days in case you needed anything." I am still overwhelmed with the caring of both the chairman and the surgeon for someone who didn't even want to admit she had hips.

We went on to Shenzhen in the south, near Hong Kong. There were many speeches and television and newspaper interviews, and everyone was operating at the highest level of inquiry and appreciation. I had one encounter that was providential. After a speech, a young couple came up, introduced themselves, thanked me, and said, "This is our daughter, Lin Youchen. We would like you to be her mentor." The father was a lawyer for the city government, the mother worked on a newspaper, and Youchen was about to begin college. I replied, "I would be honored. With e-mail we can communicate easily." We talked, then said good-bye. I didn't hear from them for six months, when I received a phone call. "Hello, this is Lin Youchen. I am in Staten Island and going to school. I am ready to be mentored." In June 2009, Youchen received her master's degree in finance from New York University, and we continue our mentoring relationship to this day.

In the intervening years, her parents, Benshu and Yixing, were able to visit their daughter in New York, and I had the privilege of bringing all three to my home in Easton, Pennsylvania, for the weekend. This small colonial town, where both George Washington and John Adams stopped at Bachman's Tavern, was as welcoming to the Lin family as Shenzhen was to me and our Leader to Leader team.

We went to Dongguan on our last day in China, and I've never received a warmer welcome or had a more responsive audience than the nine hundred business and government leaders and university students I spoke to in a beautiful new conference hall. The architecture was part of the inspiring context. On the stage where I spoke were no big posters or placards but instead two wide floor-to-ceiling blue satin panels. On one was my chart "Circular Management." On the other side of the stage was my chart "Journey to Transformation." Both were part of my speech.

When I finished speaking, the governor of the province stood beside me, pointed to the circular chart, and said, "Thank you for bringing to China the concept of roundness. The circle was a value of ancient China. The circle is a value of China, today." I can assure you that long ago, when I began throwing out the old people-in-boxes hierarchical structure and philosophy and began managing in a world that is round, using a flat, fluid, circular concept and language, I never dreamed that one day I would stand before nine hundred fellow travelers in China with congruent circles of respect, inclusion, energy unleashed—all of us speaking a common language.

In the autumn of 2009, Chairman Shao invited me to China again to help celebrate the Drucker centennial at events in China. I spoke at the Peter Drucker centennial ceremony and later on gave a talk called "Drucker and Me" and one called "Leadership Imperatives," the titles they requested, and attended two media events. Rarely have I been so inspired by such warm, responsive audiences—Chinese students, faculty, business leaders, philanthropists, philosophers, community members, and organization leaders—all celebrating the hundredth birthday of Peter Drucker, the father of modern management, with an outpouring of love and appreciation.

I was very impressed with the enormous changes in China since my last visit: the buildings, the architecture, the shops, and the obviously thriving economy. Unchanged were the Chinese courtesy, appreciation, and warm response. I was surprised by the number of participants who expressed their gratitude for my "respect" for them and their society. One man from Jilin University wrote to me, "So nice to meet you during the Drucker Centennial Forum in Beijing and Nanchang. Thank you so much for your great and moving lectures, and I really appreciate your true respect for all the people here, which is the memorable gift for us." Over and over they referred to respect, and how they valued that message.

Chairman Shao planned Drucker centennial events in four Chinese cities. From Beijing, I went to Nanchang the next day and gave a talk titled "The Leader of the Future— Imperatives of Leadership" at the Drucker Centennial Forum. From Nanchang I proceeded to Shanghai for a keynote speech to the China Executive Leadership Academy, and was greeted with the same love, enthusiasm, and determination to keep Peter Drucker's life and work alive for future leaders. Then I flew on to Hong Kong for another Drucker Forum, where I spoke on leadership and received the first China Drucker Fellow Award, presented by Bright China Group's founder, Shao Ming Lo.

The presentation was moving, personal, and inspiring. I was deeply aware of the significance of being the first honoree to receive this leadership award. I cherish that moment with one of China's greatest philanthropists and one of the world's most powerful examples of corporate social responsibility in action.

Seeing Yourself in Perspective

I am gratified that wherever I go, whatever the country, around the world, there is no strangeness. I feel that that particular place is where I am supposed to be at that moment, even when events are swirling out of control.

I happened to be attending the World Conference of Girl Guides and Girl Scouts in Iran just before the shah of Iran left the country, as the country went under martial law and antigovernment demonstrations continued around the clock. We were staying not in a hotel but in the Olympic Village, halfway between Tehran and the airport, and army trucks circled the village all night long. It was a difficult time, yet within the walls of the Olympic Village, the girls and leaders of the Girl Guides of Iran were warm and welcoming as they hosted the conference. I can never forget the marvelous young Iranian Girl Guides who were our aides during the conference, and the Girl Guide adults who welcomed us so warmly and then helped us leave on one of the last Pam Am flights to depart Iran before the government fell.

The last World Conference of Girl Guides and Girl Scouts I attended was in Kenya, not in Nairobi, but way out in the bush. The hospitality was wonderful. When it was over, our U.S. delegation of six took a hot-air balloon ride over the Serengeti. Hovering eight hundred feet in the air, we looked down at the plains below, and from horizon to horizon stretched a long black line of thousands of migrating wildebeest. As we watched, a young lioness pursued one of the small wildebeest. Just as she was ready to pounce on him, she stopped and sat down. We all cheered and decided that she was out foraging for food for her mate, as lionesses must do, and at the last minute decided, "Enough. Let him find his own food." All feeble joking aside, it was the most powerful experience, completely unlike anything I had ever encountered before—seeing the world from a new angle helps you see yourself in perspective. That is what traveling does. And every encounter widens that circle of respect for all people.

∞

After life-shaping experiences in sixty-eight countries so far, I can say I have never had a bad experience in any one of them. I've been asked, "How do you choose among all the international invitations you receive?" My reply is that I ask myself, "Are they [the organization] making a difference?" If the answer is yes, I then ask, "If I go, will I make a difference?" If the answer to the second question is also yes, I go. If there is one no, I stay home. Changing lives is the bottom line.

PART THREE

CONCERNS
AND
CELEBRATIONS

CHAPTER 13

TO SERVE IS TO LIVE

For many of us, John W. Gardner was a great hero. He served six U.S. presidents in various leadership capacities, including as secretary of health, education, and welfare; founded Common Cause and cofounded Independent Sector; and authored numerous eloquent books, including *Excellence, Self-Renewal,* and *On Leadership.* His life and language shaped our lives. In his very last speech, shortly before he died, he delivered a powerful message calling us to serve: "I keep running into highly capable people all over this country who literally never give a thought to the well-being of their community. And I keep wondering who gave them permission to stand aside! I'm asking you to issue a wake-up call to those people—a bugle call right in their ear. And I want you to tell them that this nation could die of comfortable indifference to the problems that only citizens can solve. Tell them that."

John Gardner is gone from us, yet his life and messages illuminate the darkness of our times. His call to action is more urgent than ever before.

I travel several times a week, speaking to, working with, and learning from thousands of leaders in communities here and abroad who are not guilty of "comfortable indifference." They have taken on their share of social and human challenges and are doing something about "the well-being of their community."

One powerful example is Crayons to Computers. Crayons to Computers was created by one woman as a response to the high number of Cincinnati schoolteachers who were buying school supplies out of their own pockets. The Crayons to Computers program employs inmates from twenty-three prisons around the state of Ohio to transform donated paper, felt, and other raw materials into useful classroom items, including flash cards, journals, maps, book bags, and other educational tools and incentives. The program reduces inmate idleness and fulfills community service requirements attached to certain prison sentences. Over sixty-five hundred inmates have participated in the program, and 750,000 community service hours have been spent producing $2.8 million worth of supplies made from recycled materials.

All of this because one woman decided that teachers and students deserved the supplies they needed in the schools. She mobilized unlikely partners—corporate leaders, prison wardens, and prisoners—and enriched the lives of thousands of students. Crayons to Computers is just one example of addressing "the problems that only citizens can solve."

Here's another story, one that you know is close to my heart: in Minneapolis, the local Girl Scout council has collaborated with community groups to recruit 228 Muslim girls to join local Girl Scout troops, as reported in a November 28, 2007, *New York Times* article, "To Muslim Girls, Scouts Offer a Chance to Fit In." According to the article, "Muslim girls who wear traditional dress may feel excluded from the mainstream culture, but scouting helps build bridges."

"All in all, scouting gives the girls a rare sense of belonging, troop leaders and members say," the *Times* reported. It quoted twelve-year-old Asma as saying, "It's kind of cool to say that you are a Girl Scout. It is good to have something to associate yourself with other Americans . . . . I like to be part of society. I like being able to say that I am a Girl Scout just like any other girl."

In 1912, when the Girl Scouts of the USA was founded, I am sure Juliette Low did not visualize Muslim Girl Scouts in Minnesota wearing their Girl Scout badge sashes to school over their flowing head scarves and long skirts. She and millions of Girl Scout leaders have continued the philosophy and the values of inclusion and diversity for almost a hundred years. The passion for inclusion, for serving all girls, is still pervasive today, as the *Times* article recognizes. In Minnesota, leaders of the Girl Scouts and Islamic groups reached out, collaborated, built bridges, changed lives, and strengthened the entire community.

Values are what Girl Scouting is all about. In the quaintly formal language of its Congressional Charter, Girl Scouts of the USA aims to "inspire the rising generation with the highest ideals of character, patriotism, conduct, and attainment." Stated more simply today, "Girl Scouting builds girls of courage, confidence, and character, who make the world a better place."

Whether the children were the girls of Hmong tribes who immigrated to the United States after the Vietnam war or the children of today's Muslim families in Minnesota, collaboration with schools and community agencies is a natural and time-honored response by Girl Scout volunteers and staff, who have never needed a bugle call, never suffered from "comfortable indifference."

Pillars of Democracy

So how do we mobilize our communities, our leaders, our families—all of us concerned with the health of all our children, the health of all our communities, and the health of our society? For a long time I have believed that since the beginning of our country, two institutions have sustained the democracy. One is public education. The other is the U.S. Army. Both need our passionate and generous support—now more than ever.

Our Schools

Our schools are struggling everywhere, not just in Cincinnati, where Crayons to Computers operates. I know of many other schools where the teachers are "maxed out" purchasing school supplies out of their own pockets. I asked one teacher in such a school, where I was to give the commencement speech, "Is there anything you need for Graduation Day?" He responded wistfully, "It would be nice if we could have two American flags for the kids to carry in the procession."

These are those seemingly small things a friend of a school can provide. We think back to the schools we attended as children—with adequate schoolbooks and supplies, American flags in every room—and assume that the same world

172

within those school walls exists today. For some, that is true; there are wonderful schools in our country. But there are thousands of schools crying out for help as their children fail, drop out, and join the millions of those who may never hold a steady job.

The health of our schools will determine our future. Yet we have recently learned that 50 percent of all minority children, 70 percent of all poverty-level children, and 30 percent of all American children will not receive a high school diploma. For many people, these are our invisible children.

In New York City, where our Leader to Leader Institute offices have been located since 1990, there are one million schoolchildren, and five hundred thousand of them will not receive a high school diploma. There will be no diploma, no job, no future, no hope for far too many of our children—and they are *our* children. New York is just one example. Schools all over the country are failing our children. Building more prisons is not the answer.

When I was invited to be Principal for a Day in a New York City school, I requested "a school with a few challenges and limited resources" and was given the New School for Arts and Sciences, an alternative high school for young people at risk in the South Bronx, in one of New York's poorest neighborhoods. I worked all day with classes and teachers and their remarkable principal, Gertrude Karabas.

At the end of the day, I met with the ten members of the student council and asked, "If resources could be found, what are your school's greatest needs?" Their response: "A library. We don't have one. Wouldn't it be wonderful for all the kids if we could have a library? And we need textbooks. We don't have any. Wouldn't it be wonderful if every kid could have a textbook [even though they have seven subjects]? Third: You talked to all the kids and teachers about leading beyond the walls and everybody working together to make it a better place. Could you find someone, a mentor to help us with a project so that we could make the South Bronx a better place for everyone?"

All I did was tell the story of these young leaders to friends like you, who began writing checks—so far, $25,000 for books. The school now has a library and ended up on the cover of *Time* magazine's *Time for Kids*, pictured in their own library with their own books. Textbooks are in the hands of all the students, and the then president of Junior Achievement recruited Pfizer and Verizon, who adopted the school, responding to the third expressed need. The next year, in a school that has never graduated a senior class, we graduated fifty-two students; nine of the student council members had college scholarships, and the tenth was accepted by the Air Force.

In a distressed neighborhood, in a school where the needs were great, young leaders identified three compelling needs—all to build a better school and neighborhood in the South Bronx. John Gardner would have been inspired by the example of these young citizens who did not need a bugle call.

If we look around us, we can find individuals and organizations in our own communities mobilizing to address the problems that only citizens can solve. There are vast problems and unmet needs in every community. Will we heed the call?

The U.S. Army

Our Army is an essential institution in our democracy. In the midst of a long war, with an Army that is stretched with extended tours and strained families, it is essential that we take a new look at the role of national service.

In 1998, General Dennis Reimer, chief of staff of the U.S. Army, and General Timothy Maude, then deputy chief of staff for personnel, invited me to the Pentagon to speak on leadership and diversity to the officers responsible for Army personnel. After I spoke, we had a spirited dialogue, and then a general said, "Mrs. Hesselbein, I am responsible for recruitment. We aren't getting the number of new recruits we require. If you were in charge, what would you do?"

I took "in charge" broadly and replied,

> Tomorrow morning, I would institute national and community service for every eighteen-year-old man and woman in the United States. They would serve eighteen months or two years. They could serve in one of the five branches of the military, or communities across the country could design community service programs that would bring new levels of inclusion, diversity, and engagement. They could work on the roads and bridges of the crumbling infrastructure of our country; they could move into our public schools and work in a teaching corps that would ensure that every child could read and double the number of our children receiving high school diplomas. And when their two years of service were completed, every young man and woman would be eligible for scholarships—for two years

175

of college or technical training—whatever they desired.

Our eighteen-year-olds would have found themselves, would be imbued with the spirit of service, and our country would have a new face, a new respect for all people. And all of our children would have an opportunity to learn and grow. That is my response to your question.

The general said, "Ma'am, that is the last thing I expected you to say." That was 1998. I wasn't "in charge" then nor am I now, but the needs of our schoolchildren and of our bridges, waterfronts, and road infrastructure are greater today than in 1998—and today the Army is stretched beyond reasonable limits. (We lost General Timothy Maude when the plane crashed into the Pentagon on September 11. The next month, he was to open our Conference Board – Drucker Foundation leadership conference. General John Keane spoke at the opening, and we dedicated the conference to the memory of General Maude.)

It may seem naive to ask that this new army of eighteen-year-olds adopt this new vision of serving, making the U.S. military their own. It may be naive, but it is essential. Attracting young people to military service requires more than telling the story in a new way, communicating the message of love of country and service beyond self in new and powerful ways to all of our young people. It requires tangible action demonstrating that service to the U.S. military is indeed service to the common good.

When we truly focus on the common good, service is a privilege—not a chore but a remarkable opportunity. Inspire the brightest, most articulate eighteen-year-olds to tell the story and communicate the many ways to serve. Recruitment will have a new definition, and service will have a new significance that comes from values, from the hearts our new message has touched. A program of national service will foster new alliances, new partners, and new collaborations that will inspire and support a new generation ready to serve, in the military, in our schools, restoring our roads and bridges, meeting the unmet needs across the community. All of this requires from all three sectors vision, courage, innovation, generosity, sharing, and inclusion. Shimmering far in the distance is our vision of the future: a country with citizens who care about all of its people, and young men and women called, eager to serve as leaders at every level, sustaining the democracy.

Today, many of us have a forum, a platform. How can we use our position to encourage, motivate, and inspire eighteen-year-olds to embrace national and community service? How can we mobilize colleges, universities, foundations, and citizens to say, "Yes—for two years of service, we will provide two years of the learning of your choice"? If we think this is too ambitious, too massive, or someone else's business, we need to think again. The alternatives are not pleasant to contemplate.

A powerful program of national and community service would institute such a mobilization of idealism, passion, love

177

of country, and desire to serve (with the understanding that to serve is to live) that it could transform our democracy. In five or ten years, these hundreds of thousands of young men and women who served would go on to the next adventure in learning and then become a new generation of citizens, citizens who have served their country, their communities, and their people, and who will forever sustain the democracy—a new "Greatest Generation."

How Do We Begin?

Today our U.S. Army is stretched and public education is failing millions of our children. Both are essential institutions. So we need to put the daily turmoil of political discord aside and turn our attention to providing leadership in building the healthy community—taking our personal share of the responsibility. It follows that if we fail in the support of our children in our schools and of our young men and women in our military, we must ask the question, "How can we then sustain the democracy?"

That's the big picture. We know how to lead, to mobilize, to plan, to contribute our own unique share to changing lives, building community, serving those who serve our country. But will we heed the call? If not all of us, some of us must take the lead. It's all about leadership, and knowing that to serve is to live. We can make a new beginning for our society.

You may ask, "With the needs so great, how do we begin?"

To that I answer, "You begin at the beginning." I was once caught in New York traffic on the way to the airport for a flight to Switzerland. I was thinking about the key staff members of the International Federation of Red Cross and Red Crescent Societies with whom I would be working in Geneva the next week. They were coming from their posts all over the world and from many cultures, races, languages, and backgrounds. These were the men and women who are first into Rwanda, Darfur, Haiti, and other devastated areas, and the last to leave—all of them committed to the International Red Cross mission: "To serve the most vulnerable."

I was thinking about how I could open my session on leadership in a way that would connect with the richest mix of cultures, races, and ethnicities, with people who were mostly working in English but processing what was said into another language. I looked beside me at a bus that also was stalled in traffic, and on the side of the bus was a big advertisement, but not the usual ones for Calvin Klein or Ralph Lauren. On this huge white placard were just four lines:

> To achieve greatness:
> Start where you are,
> Use what you have,
> Do what you can.
> —ARTHUR ASHE

It was providential. I was moved and inspired. So I took this message from the distinguished American sportsman, humanitarian, and author at the tragic end of his life, dying of an HIV-tainted blood transfusion, to people who deal every day with the most tragic human conditions and circumstances, often with massive needs, limited supplies, and too few workers.

179

Ashe's message traveled back around the world when we said good-bye. It gave change a human face and challenge a human dimension. You will note that Ashe did not say, "To just get along . . ." He said, "To achieve greatness." The language of leadership.

When I am working with MBA students at Harvard, or on other campuses where the dialogue is vigorous and enlightening, invariably students will say something like this: "But we will be middle management. How can we make the changes you talk about if we are not at the top?" I reply, "You can begin where you are, start where you are. Whatever your job, you can bring new insight and new leadership to your team and your group."

Start where you are in your own community. For example, adopting a school is not difficult. A little help—books for libraries, ink cartridges for computer printers, school supplies, career fairs—can change the lives of these children, their schools, and their communities. All of us can find our place in serving the common good in our own way, making our own contribution to a new and vibrant and caring society that only citizens can restore. "Start where you are."

Rock Climbers

In the very magnitude and complexity of our lives as leaders in tenuous times, there are the most magnificent, most compelling, most significant opportunities to lead, find solutions, and rebuild the healthy community.

For leaders in all three sectors determined to help build the healthy, diverse, inclusive community that cares about all its people, there is a new appreciation that when we build the healthy community, it is for the greater good. And even for a leader with little concern about the greater good, there is the reality that a sick and ailing community cannot produce the healthy, energetic, and productive workforce our enterprises demand if they are to be viable and even present a decade hence.

If the mountain of challenges we face seems formidable, let's look at some of those "rock climbers" who are starting where they are, using what they have, and doing what they can to build a better future.

A small group of university presidents from the United States held a retreat and chose the University of Oxford as the place to gather for their "Oxford Conclave on Global Ethics and the Changing University Presidency." I had the honor of joining these visionaries to speak on leadership and ethics, then to participate in the discussion and help facilitate for four days. It was inspiring to see this small group of presidents not content to deal only with the daily challenges of their own university leadership but instead moving beyond the walls to examine two universal issues. I still hear from the university presidents and the students from the United States who were participants in the Oxford Conclave.

Rock climbers are found everywhere. Shortly after Katrina devastated New Orleans, three remarkable college students from Duke University, seeing thousands of people stranded by inadequate rescue efforts, decided to take action. These rock climbers, as reported by South Carolina's *Herald-Sun*, drove their small Hyundai twelve hours to reach New Orleans, posed as journalists to slip inside the flooded city, and evacuated three women and a man. The next day they went back in and rescued three more people in their small car. Seven people who weren't receiving help from authorities were saved and put on a bus to Texas. Rock climbers see a need and take action. They lead by example.

The people left behind in New Orleans were rock climbers as well, even as the waters surged around them. Reports from two California paramedics who were stranded by the flooding tell of maintenance workers who used a fork lift to carry the sick and disabled; of engineers who rigged up generators and kept them running; of nurses who took over for mechanical ventilators and spent many hours manually breathing for unconscious patients; of mechanics who helped hot-wire any car they could find to carry people to safety; and of food service workers who scoured the commercial kitchens to improvise communal meals for hundreds of those stranded. These are profound examples of the power of human spirit, reminders of another powerful insight from Arthur Ashe: "True heroism is not the urge to surpass all others at whatever cost, but the urge to serve others at whatever cost."

It will take all of us to build healthy communities. Together, we can change the world—bring a new world to all our children. We just need to start where we are.

If in his dying days Arthur Ashe could care enough to leave his message for us, can we do less? What message will we leave?

CHAPTER 14

SEEING AND LISTENING

As I have mentioned, the person who had the greatest impact on me was my grandmother. People always expect me to talk about John W. Gardner, Peter Drucker, Warren Bennis, or Jim Collins—all the great thought leaders who have been part of my journey. They all have had a powerful impact on my life and my work. Yet from my first consciousness of relations with other people, my quiet, lovely grandmother has been my role model. Mama Wicks listened very carefully. With grandchildren six or seven years old, she looked into our eyes and she listened as though it was the most important thing she could be doing at that moment, and she never cut us off. We finished our little story, whatever it was. She listened to us with total concentration and warm response, and we learned to listen because we wanted to be like Mama Wicks. That kind of sensitivity and appreciation of others was a very important lesson, one I learned very early. Now and all through my life, I have often gone back and thought about a saying she encouraged me to memorize when I was a child.

When she was a little girl, her family had a lumber mill back in the mountains of western Pennsylvania, where they made barrel staves. The family built this little lumber mill long before the Civil War began, in the 1840s. Nearby was a one-room schoolhouse that she and her father and grandfather had attended. Above the blackboard was a maxim that could have been from a McGuffey Reader; it had always been there. It was this maxim she had me memorize: "If wisdom's ways you would wisely seek, these five things observe with care: of whom you speak, to whom you speak, how, when, and where." I memorized that when I was eight years old. Years later I have to smile: the only time I ever get into trouble is when I forget my grandmother's advice about "these five things."

The Art of Listening

I thought of my grandmother again recently when I was interviewed by a writer working on an article on "the listening leader." Listening is an art. When people are speaking, they require our undivided attention. We focus on them; we listen very carefully. We listen to the spoken words and the unspoken messages. This means looking directly at the person, eyes connected; we forget we have a watch, just focusing for that moment on that person. It's called respect, it's called appreciation—and it's called leadership.

Listening is one of the most effective ways of learning what the customer values. We need to listen to all our customers, all the people within the organization and those beyond the walls of the organization. And through listening we learn what they value. This is a critical skill, and openness to others is an indispensable attitude. When we learn to listen openly, without reservation, it brings us to a higher level of understanding and appreciation of our own people and of those we can reach beyond the walls.

I learned this lesson very early in my work with Girl Scouts. Girl Scouts learn through doing. In today's world, where there are so many voices clamoring to be heard, Girl Scouts of the USA has always been wisest when it stops, listens, and then moves ahead truly understanding the needs, spoken and unspoken, of girls in today's world. That is when we have done our best.

Listening to girls begins, of course, in the Girl Scout troop or group. The way a leader listens can make a world of difference to a young girl who is just learning to share her ideas. Whether or not you agree with the idea, it must be treated with respect. A thoughtful and caring response may help the girl clarify her own thinking; it will surely create one of those wonderful moments when girls learn from and through their leader. What applies to girls and their troop leader applies equally to managers and their leaders. Leaders who are too impatient to listen, who insist on telling, will struggle to build enthusiastic, committed teams.

Being Heard

Communication is not just saying something; it is being heard. Because communication is being heard, the leader consciously asks, "Am I getting through? Is my message being heard?" How many times have we heard a leader complain, "I've told him and I've told him, but he just doesn't get it"? The leader was talking yet not being heard, was not communicating. When this happens, when it's obvious we're not being heard, it's time to stop talking and listen; it's time to deliver the message a different way. Listening is the essential element of effective leadership.

How do we foster listening in others? Listening is not a solo performance; it is a connection, and is most successful when circular. I listen, you respond; you listen, I respond; and somehow in that magic circle of communication, we hear each other's message. The Great Stone Face is not exactly the most conducive face for good listeners; so we respond expressively.

The writer interviewing me about listening asked what would be the one most important element, the one piece of advice I could share. As I thought of the management teams I've been part of, in which positive feedback was key to growth and productive relationships, and thought through all the aspects of listening and of communication, rising to the top as number one was "banish the *but*." If we want people to listen, we must banish "but" from our vocabulary. How many times have we had someone tell us how well we performed— and we were feeling good about the feedback, listening carefully—then we heard "but," and the positive, energizing part of the feedback was lost in the "but" and what followed it. "But" is nobody's friend—listener or speaker. "And" provides the graceful transition, the nonthreatening bridge to mutual appreciation, the communication that builds effective relationships. Replacing "but" with "and" is the best advice I could give to the leader who listens and wants others to listen with an open mind.

Believing the quality and character of a leader determines the performance and the results, the success of our leadership depends on how effectively we mobilize our people around mission and values and vision and how effectively all of our people listen to the customer. We are most successful when the communication is circular.

Whispers of Our Lives

There is another kind of listening—listening to our inner selves. Listening to the whispers of our lives is critical; if we fail to do so, our lives are diminished. We never reach the levels we could in understanding ourselves or in strengthening our relationships with others. Three kinds of whispers speak to us if we listen. First are the whispers of the body, when our bodies try to tell us that something is not quite right. The more intellectual we are, the more we tend to ignore the whispers of our bodies. Then one day an illness emerges, and we can go back to that day when there was this whisper and we blocked or ignored it. Second are whispers of the heart, of all the people we love and who love us, of our relationships. Third are the whispers of the spirit, however we define our faith, that inner spirit—those quiet whispers that can comfort, heal, inspire.

∞

I think again of my grandmother who, even as she listened to her children and her grandchildren, told us stories about the seven Pringle brothers who went off to the Civil War, and stories about their wives who were left behind to take care of children and farms. She talked in such a compelling way that we listened and remembered her stories long, long after she was gone and we were grown.

187

As we peer ahead, the future seems ever more tenuous. A world of increasing polarization, conflict, and war requires new levels of listening from all of us wherever we are, in whatever we are doing. At times, the news we hear will be unwelcome and worrisome. In those cases, we must listen ever more carefully, ever more calmly: shooting the messenger is never an option. When times are difficult, the art and discipline of effective communication become even more essential. Listening is the key for leaders who would be heard.

Seeing Things Whole

Listening is not enough: we also need to see. It is not as simple as it seems. We can all look out the window and see if it is sunny or cloudy. But few of us can, like Peter Drucker, "simply look out the window and see what is visible but not yet seen." We become so focused on obvious details—quarterly results, measures of productivity, and the like—that we fail to see the forest for the trees. We fail to see things whole, placing details in their proper perspective.

"Focus on the bottom line" is drilled into many potential leaders, who then lose their way on the journey to significant and effective leadership. Certainly leaders need to manage the financial aspects of the organization with great effectiveness, but if we do not see the enterprise whole—extending from passion for the mission, values that are lived and embodied in all we do, the customer who is listened to, and partners whose collaboration is essential for our work, to the vision of the future that shimmers in the distance—we fail. Pulling out one piece, one action, one aspect of the leadership challenge is like playing a one-string guitar—noise but not much music.

Peter Drucker's admonition, "Focus, focus, focus," does not negate the imperative of seeing the organization whole. Indeed, we can see the significant priorities clearly only when we see the organization complete and intact, embedded in the world at large. Only by seeing things whole can we understand and articulate to others *why* we focus on our few significant priorities. Only by seeing things whole can we recognize when continued relevance and viability demand that we *change* our priorities.

From Hierarchy to Wholeness

When we see the organization whole and when our goals, objectives, and actions describe in a powerfully inclusive, embracing way the future we will bring alive, then all within the walls—as well as those we serve beyond the walls and those future customers we will find—will partner with us on our journey. This integrated wholeness—everything building on, flowing to and from in a circular movement—becomes a remarkable strategy for ensuring organizational relevance far into the future.

Seeing things whole is difficult in the old hierarchy. People in squares and rectangles have to struggle to move across the organization, to function in teams and groups, to carry their own share of the big picture. More and more leaders are moving the enterprise away from the old boxes and toward meeting the challenge of managing in a world that is round, as I've discussed elsewhere in this book. Seeing the organization whole and as flexible, fluid, and circular moves us into the community of the future.

Seeing Life Whole

In the end, seeing things whole is not just the imperative of business, government, and social sector leaders; the overarching, overriding imperative of seeing things whole rests with you and me. Seeing our lives whole is an even greater challenge than seeing our world of work whole.

How many times have we heard and talked about work – life balance? We continually strive to find enough time for family, friends, the people we love and who love us, and the colleagues who share our passion for the mission and vision of the future of the enterprise. And then we try to make room for that further dimension, where we try to make a difference, work to change lives in the organizations we choose to serve, volunteer in community efforts to move beyond the walls and build the healthy, inclusive community that cares about all its people.

Add staying an informed citizen, twenty laps in the pool, and running through Central Park at dawn, and we carry a big basket. How do we balance ourselves in this miraculous wholeness with rich and varied dimensions of family, friends, colleagues, careers, service, physical and psychic energy, spiritual and intellectual calling?

I remember in the early days of the Drucker Foundation when I asked Lewis Platt, then chairman of Hewlett-Packard, to write an article for our book *The Organization of the Future*. One might expect this great leader to write about cyberspace and the technology of the future. Instead his response was, "If you don't mind, I would like to write about employee work – life balance, the greatest challenge to American corporations. If we ever get it right, it will be win-win for everyone."

I've never forgotten our conversation. I carry his response around with me as I try to find the answers to work – life balance, to seeing life whole.

It is sad when highly successful corporate leaders tell me that they were so busy making it that they really didn't have time for their own children, but now they are having a wonderful time with their grandchildren. That isn't good enough. For leaders everywhere, our common challenge is to see life whole—wherever we are on our journey.

The Big Picture

We are all challenged to lead in an era of far greater discontinuity than we experienced ten or twenty years ago. In this world, successful leaders need to communicate even more clearly with the people of the organization, the customers of the organization, and the many publics they engage—always reflecting in what they say and do that communication is not saying something but being heard. Here the ability to distill language is one of the most effective skills the leader of the future can perfect. One sentence, one paragraph, one page often command far more attention than reams of explanation and analysis.

Effective leaders practice the art of listening and practice Peter Drucker's admonition to "think first, speak last." Leaders who are healers and unifiers use listening to include, not exclude; they build consensus, appreciate differences, and find common concepts, common language, and common ground.

Seeing and listening go together. Facing challenges, fostering community involvement, collaborating, and focusing on future relevance and significance are critical for leaders who see things whole. These leaders put away the magnifying glass, step back from the details, and engage in the larger world. Because they engage with others and listen carefully, they can see through more than one pair of eyes, using the viewpoints of others to enlarge their own perspective. Those who see the organization, the community, and the society whole are the leaders of the future who in the end will sustain the democracy. That's the big picture of listening and seeing.

CHAPTER 15

LEADERS OF THE FUTURE

This is a time of testing for leaders, who will need the courage to lead in a period of great divisiveness. Who are the leaders of the future who embody the values, principles, and philosophy needed to lead from the front, right into this turbulent future, in a world at war? Some of an older generation warn ominously of a coming leadership vacuum. The CEOs and other senior leaders wringing their hands over the search for qualified leaders to succeed them seem to have concluded that future high-potential leaders are rare.

Some lament, "When in our world will we ever see another generation like 'the Greatest Generation'?" The stories of the generation that carried us through World War II are part of the culture and history of our own families and of our country. From General Marshall and General Eisenhower to every soldier, sailor, marine, airman, and coast guardsman, to the brave men and women who kept the nation's mills, factories, and farms supplying all the materials—all put service above self. Americans at home participated in the sacrifice; they all became part of that storied generation.

Today it is a different world. I travel every week, I listen more than I speak, and I read everything I can; and many reports indicate that today we are experiencing the highest level of cynicism and the lowest level of trust in our institutions that have ever been measured. Yet I am very positive about the future, and not just because my blood type is B positive.

I get my hope, my energy, and my faith in the future from the new generation of students on college and university campuses at the University of Pittsburgh, the U.S. Military Academy at West Point, the Air Force Academy, and many others. I sense that this is a different generation from some previous ones—far less cynical and more committed to serving and to making a difference, despite the reports.

The Crucible Generation

The current generation is vastly different from earlier cohorts. The Millennials, Gen Y—whatever you choose to call them—have high expectations; live in the world of technology; value diversity and inclusion; are open-minded, performance and results driven, and globally astute; and accept their responsibility for the society. Solid research has been conducted and much has been written about today's university students, for whom leadership and civic engagement are indispensable partners in their journey to significance and service. Warren Bennis calls this generation "the crucible generation."

A range of economic and social influences have shaped the attitudes, beliefs, and expectations of this emerging generation. A recent *USA Today* study found that even though jobs are scarce and money is tight, conditions have not stopped the millennial generation from helping others. Young adults who grew up in the shadow of the 9/11 attacks, saw the wreckage of hurricane Katrina, and searched for jobs during a recession are volunteering at home and abroad in record numbers. The Millennials, the generation that learned in school to serve as well as to read and write, became the first global Internet explorers as they pioneered social networking for favorite causes at home. Students on campuses here and abroad view community service as part of their DNA. In every speech I make, I say "to serve is to live," words that are exemplified by the generation that is currently on campuses and entering the workforce. In their messages back to me, they often end with those same words.

I spend one-third of my time on college and university campuses. I do this for myself, for when I leave these campuses, I am filled with hope. There is something special about this generation of young leaders. I see in their principled, ethical, courageous leadership their definition of the leaders of the future, which they just happen to be.

Recent solid research shows that the current generation on college campuses resembles the students of the 1930s and 1940s. Could it be possible that twenty years from now we will say, "Once again, the Greatest Generation"? All this begins with you and me—encouraging, supporting, inspiring, and enabling today's young men and women to put service above self.

Perhaps you and I, knowing as well as we do our own times—with all its challenges, disparities, ambiguities, and even dangers to our people, communities, and society—perhaps we will find fresh hope in the leadership of this new generation. I see in "the Greatest Generation" that served our country long ago the model and inspiration for today's young leaders to serve in new and different ways in a future we cannot yet define.

John Gardner might have been speaking directly to us about this generation of emerging leaders when he wrote in his book *Self-Renewal*, "Instead of giving young people the impression that their task is to stand a dreary watch over the ancient values, we should be telling them ... that it is their task to re-create these values continuously in their own behavior.... We should be telling them that each generation refights the crucial battles and either brings new vitality to the ideals or allows them to decay."

Express Yourself

Not all agree on a description of emerging leaders, yet there is agreement on the significance of these young leaders in redefining the future of the organization and of the society. One of the exciting parts of my life these days is the number of invitations I receive to engage in dialogue with small groups of these young men and women. I'm finding their questions far more exciting than my responses. These are some of the questions they ask:

How did you get started?
When did you know you would be a leader?
What makes you so positive?
Where do you get your energy?
How do you elevate others while accomplishing your mission?

How do you find a mentor?

How do you get into the social sector as a career?

How do you find a community project?

What was the worst bad day in your work with the Girl Scouts?

To that last question, I reply, "I never had a bad day in those five thousand days I served with Girl Scouts of the USA. I had some tough ones, but never a bad day." In answer to the first two questions, I often quote Warren Bennis.

In my last year with the Girl Scouts of the USA, Warren published a book, *On Becoming a Leader*, in which he profiled twenty-three leaders after interviewing one hundred. The book was so successful that he made a videotape, *The Leader Within*, with three leaders from the book: Max De Pree, chairman of Herman Miller; General Dave Palmer, superintendent of West Point; and me.

Of the leaders profiled in the book, the three of us seemed a strange and wondrous choice for a videotape designed to train managers in the corporate world. What could office furniture, cadets at West Point, and the Girl Scouts have in common? The three of us were filmed separately in three parts of the country, without scripts, and I really wondered how it would all mesh. It was amazing how Warren found powerful commonalities, common lessons in leadership, among our three very different lives. The video highlighted four key elements: commitment to mission, self-knowledge, communicating vision, and personal integrity—four fundamentals of leadership. At the end, Warren looks into the camera and says, "These three people never started out to become leaders. They began by expressing themselves in their work, and along the way, they became leaders." I still look at that video from long ago and marvel at how Warren then and to this day distills language and wisdom as few writers or philosophers can.

His insight resonates with young people on college campuses, the leaders of the future who are wondering how and when this moment will happen, the moment when they are recognized as leaders. When they ask me, "How will I know when I get there?" I share Warren's wisdom: "You begin by expressing yourself in your work, and along the way you become a leader." Somehow to them, "Expressing yourself in your work" sounds reasonable and attainable. Warren's wisdom helps all of us realize that becoming a leader is not a destination, but a long and exuberant journey.

Of course, to young leaders of the future, or to leaders at any point along the way, the questions are, "Who is that leader within? If I am expressing myself in my work, what are my ethics, my beliefs, my values, my philosophy? What do I believe? What do I value? Is my behavior consistent with my beliefs?"

If observers say of us, "They expressed themselves in their work, and along the way they became leaders," then "know thyself" is a critical component.

Mentoring

All of us, we leaders of the present, need to appreciate the privilege, the imperative of mentoring emerging leaders. I mentor three: I've spent ten years with the New York University graduate student from China whom I mentioned in Chapter Twelve, whose parents I met in Shenzhen; ten years with a young Coast Guard officer, now working in the world of diplomacy; and on occasion, a young lawyer from the South. What do I learn from this experience with these three young women? That mentoring is circular. I learn as much from them as they do from me. Mentoring is a leadership privilege.

I make time to meet with young leaders who want to come to my office in New York just to talk, to connect. And sometimes they introduce me as their mentor. I'm not their mentor in the strictest sense, but we are fellow travelers, sharing the journey. Gloria Fahlikman, my indispensible executive assistant, always finds time on our overstretched calendar for these young leaders who, for a brief moment, remind us of why we do what we do.

Sometimes in speeches, or when working with university students, I state the U.S. Army Warrior Ethos:

I will always place the mission first.
I will never accept defeat.
I will never quit.
I will never leave a fallen comrade.

Some of these students translate the Warrior Ethos into their own language, their own situation, and their own lives. The ethos is not about the U.S. Army. It is about them.

One inspiring example of a young leader who gives me hope for the future is Captain Ben Tolle, graduate of West Point Class of 2005, who was commanding a company of young soldiers in Baghdad. The e-mail messages I received from him had no complaints, only praise for the remarkable young men and women in his command. One day, an e-mail arrived from Ben in Baghdad, saying he was coming home and would be stationed near Nashville for a while:

> Dear Frances:
> I am nearly out of Iraq and complete with my first deployment. Do you know of any nonprofit where I could volunteer a couple of afternoons or evenings a week in Nashville? Helping work events, fundraising, or planning?

Of course his e-mail and my response went immediately to several great nonprofit organizations in Nashville. And I just happened to be speaking in Nashville a short time later to 250 community leaders. Have you any doubt about what was the most inspiring part of my speech? Or that Captain Ben's spirit—as a leader of the present, a leader of the future—stays with me? He expresses himself in his work, knowing that leadership is a journey, not a destination.

Faces in the Crowd

Let me tell you one more story of a courageous young soldier, a leader of the future. Traveling twice a week, speaking here or abroad, lands me in many airports, with lots of waiting in long lines, yet I often see young faces in the crowd that give me hope. Whenever I see one of our soldiers in uniform in an airport, I always go up and say, "I hope you understand how much we appreciate you and what you are doing for all of us and our country." Invariably, the reply is "Thank you, ma'am" or "Just doing my job." So many of our service people are so young, they touch my heart.

A while ago, I was in the Dallas airport, changing planes to go on to an engagement in the Texas Panhandle, where I was speaking the next day. Walking toward the gate, I noticed a very young soldier, went up to him, and said, "Sir, I hope you understand how much we appreciate you and what you are doing for all of us and our country." He looked surprised and said, "Thank you, ma'am."

When I got to the gate, there he was again, waiting to board the flight I was on. So I walked over, sat beside him for a moment, and said that I hoped he was on leave, going home. He told me he had been flying for twenty-five hours, from Baghdad to Shannon (Ireland) and now Dallas, with an hour to wait for the flight to his hometown. He had a two-week leave at home, so I gave him my card and asked him to e-mail me his APO address when he returned, saying I would send him some things to read. He said he would like that, but that it would be three weeks before I would hear from him. Then he put in my hand a rumpled Iraqi bill—5,000 dinars. When I said I couldn't take his money, he smiled and said, "Ma'am, I want you to have it; it's not even worth a dollar." I told him I would frame it and put it in my office as a reminder of him and all our young soldiers.

I thanked him and went back to my seat, thinking of this eighteen-year-old gunner, working in 125-degree heat in Iraq with no complaints. After a moment, I trotted back and pressed a coin in his hand. General William "Kip" Ward had given it to me several weeks before when I spoke to the

Military Child Education Coalition conference in Houston, and I said, "I have been carrying this with me for good luck. Now I want you to carry it for good luck." He said, "Oh ma'am, I can't accept this. It's a general's coin." (Military leaders, at times, have special coins that they present in recognition of an individual's contribution.) I said, "I have accepted your Iraqi money, which I will cherish always. You have to accept General Ward's coin. I know he would be honored that I've given it to you." He tucked it away in his pocket.

When we landed, the young soldier's family was waiting: mother, father, grandparents, and two little brothers about five and seven, dressed in the same 1st Infantry uniform he was wearing. I've never seen such hugs. Two little soldiers welcomed their big brother home for two weeks—while one little brother was in his arms, the other was hugging the young soldier's leg. It was a poignant moment for me, watching a tired young soldier, modest, quiet, no complaints, just doing his job. And he is carrying my coin for good luck.

Faces in the crowd have an amazing way of emerging in their own way, all of them making their unique contributions to our world. The most vivid faces in my crowds are those of college and university students here and abroad, and young soldiers just doing their jobs. They inspire me. Thomas Friedman wrote about this cohort in a recent *New York Times* op-ed piece, calling them "the Quiet Americans." In his article he observes, "And that can-do-will-do spirit is a good thing, because we will need it to preserve our democracy from those who want to steal the openness and optimism that make democracy work."

Light a Fire

The emerging leaders I encounter are sending us a powerful message: one of building trust, of ethics in action, of the power of diversity, of inclusion, of courage, of celebrating the intellect, and of leading from the front into an uncertain future. We'll be supporting them, cheering them on, and, in the end, following them, for they are our leaders of the future. My message to them is, "We look to you to take the lead, to lead beyond the walls, to serve as a model of ethical global citizenship and an example of the power of education. As William Butler Yeats wrote long ago, 'Education is not the filling of a pail, but the lighting of a fire.' You light a fire."

CHAPTER 16

CONCLUSION: SHINE A LIGHT

braham Lincoln is my favorite historical figure; he gave moral leadership to a nation divided, and rose to be the leader the country required in a bloody and violent period. President Lincoln understood the power of communication and the use of spare and compelling language. He would choose a few paragraphs to deliver his message, not pages of verbose prose. The Gettysburg Address, for example, was a masterpiece of concise communication.

Framed on my desk are five lines by President Lincoln:

I am not bound to win,
But I am bound to be true.
I am not bound to succeed,
But I am bound to live
Up to the light I have.

President Lincoln's words are sobering and inspiring at the same time. We all need to do our best to live up to the light we have. Remember the song, "This little light of mine, I'm going to let it shine...?? That song, and the idea that each of us shines a light, have a heartwarming history for me, one that involves thousands of people.

Jim Collins, author of the best sellers *Built to Last, Good to Great*, and *How the Mighty Fall*, and I were invited to speak on leadership at a leadership excellence conference where there would be fifty-five thousand people participating by satellite from universities and conference centers all over the world, and twenty-two thousand present, live in Atlanta. Jim and I were each invited to speak on leadership. He called me and said, "Instead of your giving a speech on leadership, then my giving a speech on leadership, let's do a dialogue." Of course when Jim Collins suggests anything, I sign on.

He said, "This is how I see it. I'll go out on that big empty stage and talk about the Level 5 leader, then I'll talk about a particular Level 5 leader. Then I'll bring you on stage. We'll sit on two small chairs on that big stage and just talk about leadership. Would you like to know the questions I'm going to ask you?"

I thought a moment and decided it would be far more spontaneous, far more exciting, if I didn't know, so I said no. Later I decided I was out of my mind, but we followed the course I chose in that exuberant moment.

The day of the conference came, and Mikhail Gorbachev, Donald Trump, Ken Blanchard, and others on the program spoke. Then came the Jim – Frances moment. Backstage, before we went on, Jim said to me, not "Break a leg" or "You'll be great," but in a quiet voice, "We will shine a light." That flowed into me. I floated out on the stage when he introduced me, and I never had a more exhilarating moment than that "shine a light dialogue" with one of the greatest thought leaders of our time. It must have been effective; in the evaluations of that daylong list of remarkable speakers, our Jim Collins session was number one. I've never had a more deeply satisfying experience. I present an edited version of our dialogue here.

Jim Collins Interviews Frances Hesselbein at the Living Leadership Conference, Atlanta, Georgia, October 20, 2004

JIM COLLINS (JC): When Frances Hesselbein became chief executive of the Girl Scouts in 1976, it was the most perilous time in the organization's history—declining market share, dissatisfied customers, economic weakness, and even hostile takeover threats. As John Bryne wrote in *Business Week*, "lurking in the corner like a corporate raider" was the Boy Scouts of America, which had launched a feasibility study of extending membership to girls. I just really wonder what would have happened had there been a hostile takeover of the Girl Scouts.

She walked into a situation of eight straight years of declining membership. It had gone from great to good. And she came in as a consummate Level 5, ambitious for the cause of the Girl Scouts. "We are here to make girls strong. We are here to develop young girls into competent women. That is what we're here to do." But she had a key insight. The way we've done it is outdated. We used to define making girls ready for the future as making them ready for marriage. We gave them the merit badges in sewing and cleaning and whatever.

But what about the skills that would allow you to be a competent, independent, strong woman in today's world? How about the math proficiency badge? How about the accounting merit badge? And what about all the girls who aren't white? The Girls Scouts at that time served mainly white girls. And Frances said, "No. We must have every part of society. We must have *all* girls be strong. We must become more inclusive."

So what she did was, she said, "We are going to maintain our values, but we are going to change the practices of the Girls Scouts and make them relevant to today's world, but never lose our principles."

Under her leadership, membership grew to 2.25 million girls, and a workforce mainly of volunteers that was 780,000 when she left. She received the Presidential Medal of Freedom in 1998, our nation's highest civilian honor.

But the signature of a Level 5 is what happens after you leave. Anyone who leaves an organization that declines is not Level 5. What happened? The great leader left, and the Girl Scouts grew to four million members. The great leader left, nearly one million volunteers. And now she's the chief leader of the Leader to Leader Institute, whose very mission is the development of Level 5 in our society ... creating leaders in all sectors.

We have with us here, and I would like to bring out and have a conversation with her, one of my heroes, someone who I love very much, Frances Hesselbein. She makes me happy. She's happy, too.

FRANCES HESSELBEIN (FH): Yes, very happy.

JC: The place I'd like to begin is, why at the time of life that you could have relaxed did you take on the burden of the Girl Scouts?

FH: Burden? Don't be ridiculous. The most remarkable organization in the world. The most remarkable people. It was the perfect organization, and it needed to take the lead right into the future.

JC: Can you tell us a little bit about how you made the Girl Scouts relevant to today's world without giving up the values?

FH: Not *I*. *We*. You don't sit at a desk in New York and say, "Let there be relevance" or "Let there be diversity." No. It happens on the ground, in the neighborhoods where the people are. And those remarkable people ... together we fashioned a vision. And we all caught fire with a powerful, distilled mission. It had nothing to do with bigness. Bigness doesn't inspire anyone. It had to do with helping each girl reach her own highest potential. We knew why we do what we do. And that was step one. We mobilized around vision and mission, had a couple powerful goals that they helped develop. It was theirs.

JC: There's a wonderful story that I came across in learning about those years. A *New York Times* reporter had you at lunch and asked what it was like to be on top of an organization like this. You had a wonderful response which was kind of like dealing with a child that didn't quite get it. You proceeded to quietly rearrange all the food at the table. I don't know if you guys ate after this, but basically you created a series of concentric circles. And in the middle of all these connecting plates and forks and so on, you pointed to the middle and said, "I'm not on top of anything. I'm in the middle of a connected web."

FH: Right.

JC: Can you tell us about that, and, in particular, your feelings about words like *top* and *bottom* and *level*.

FH: When I found myself in my first professional job as the CEO of the Talus Rock Girl Scout council in the mountains of western Pennsylvania, I looked at those people in boxes on that chart, and I thought, "No, this isn't right for us." So, at my kitchen table in Johnstown, I put cups and glasses and made two concentric circles with the leader in the center. I threw out the old hierarchical language, no top, no bottom, up, down, top, bottom, superior, subordinate. No one has ever said, "I can't wait to be a subordinate." When you throw out the language of the old hierarchy, and you take people out of those boxes, and you put them in a circle, you release the human spirit, you release the energy.

It worked in little Johnstown, Pennsylvania. So when I arrived in New York, I carried circular management with me. It worked just as well for a very large organization. When you throw out the language of the old hierarchy, it's amazing what it does for the organization because people will move across. You don't say, "Well, I will send the message down." Never.

JC: I'm struck by, even today in 2004, how often we hear words like "top," "down," "work for." Right? All kinds of things. We need to watch ourselves. How often do we use language that is essentially demeaning?

FH: Yes. And you see, if one of your passionate values is inclusion, then you use the language of inclusion. So, it's "ours." When you think of all the ways we separate ourselves through language, and then we use language that includes, that embraces, it's amazing what can happen. You find leaders at every level.

JC: One of the things that I was commenting on during the presentation but I wanted to ask you specifically about is that in the leadership roles you've had, you've been in more what I would call a legislative role ... having to lead without having the advantage of concentrated executive power. A CEO can just make a decision. But in most situations, in fact, that's use of power, not leadership.

And the question I have for you is, what have you learned about how to get the right decisions to happen when you don't have the concentrated power to make the decisions happen?

FH: You have the power of mission, the power of shared values, the power of language. You don't give orders. You share. What kind of results do you get from a dispirited workforce where "this is the order of the day, now get it done"? It's our shared work. And they are involved in the decisions that affect them. And the results, the productivity soars.

Peter Drucker says corporations today will have to learn to lead knowledge workers the way social sector organizations lead volunteers. It's that simple.

JC: In fact, it's interesting. We tend to think the social sector needs to recruit leadership talent from the business sector. But, as you and I have talked, maybe it should go the other direction because the corporate sector is increasingly more complex. Those in the social sector have learned to manage that complexity and to lead without power.

One of the things that we have observed that Level 5 leaders do is they practice a peculiar form of discipline. Most people think that discipline is doing. Right? But real discipline is not found in your to-do list. It's in having a stop-doing list. And in knowing what not to do. That is discipline. Most of us lead busy but undisciplined lives.

You have always been an artful user of the stop-doing list and the not-to-do list. The question I have is when there are opportunities where people are asking you or your organization to do good things, but they're not right, how do you say no with grace?

FH: You're looking at the mission, and you have only one question. If we do this, will it further the mission? If the answer is no or maybe, you find the loveliest way to say thank you very much, but at this time we have to focus on x, y, z, but we're grateful that you brought it to us.

JC: Your cardinal rule number one, as I understand it, is leadership is first about who you are.

FH: How to be.

JC: Not first what you do. Can you help us understand the Hesselbein law of leadership?

FH: Absolutely. All of us, I believe, have to define leadership on our own terms. I couldn't quote Peter Drucker and Warren Bennis forever . . . I had to have my own definition. And, finally, out of all the introspection, also known as agonizing, it came. Leadership is a matter of how to be, not how to do.

You and I spend most of our lives learning how to do and teaching others how to do. Yet we know in the end it's the quality and character of the leader that determines the performance, results. That has guided me for twenty-five years. And I never have found any reason to shift my gears.

JC: You once said something to me which stuck with me, which is that the greatest gift a leader gives to its organization is how you leave. Can you help us understand that?

FH: Yes. I think from the day we go into the job we start thinking about how and when we will leave, because it isn't about us; it's about how we're going to leave that organization, that institution, the enterprise, even better than we found it. And this isn't a public pronouncement ... this is very internal and very personal. You have goals for the organization, what you hope that marvelous, wonderful organization will achieve. And you keep testing it along the way. It doesn't mean you don't shift your gears. When I took the job, I anticipated being there three years, and I left thirteen years later. But all the time, I kept thinking, "When is the right time to leave, for the organization?" So, on January 31, 1989, I said to the national board and the national staff, "In exactly one year from today I am going to leave, and together we will build the most remarkable example, model, of leadership transition the country's ever seen."

So, we developed the model, it had four phases, it was everybody's baby, it wasn't just my leaving. It was our year of leadership transition. And my last year was the most exuberant year of my thirteen years. That's what every leader should be able to say.

And yet we look out there, we see the landscape of corporate America, or the other two sectors, littered with careers of leaders who didn't know when or how to leave. So this is a leadership imperative.

JC: Do you think most leave too soon, or overstay their usefulness?

FH: More of us stay too long, I believe.

JC: Leader to Leader, your organization now, I'm sure you're thinking ahead to what it grows into beyond you. What is the mission of Leader to Leader Institute, and how will it make the world better forever?

FH: We have a short, powerful mission statement. You can't know Peter Drucker and have a mission statement that doesn't fit on a T-shirt. So ours is "To strengthen the leadership of the social sector ..." and then I quietly add "... and their partners in business and government." And everything is focused on leadership. How do we strengthen the leadership of this indispensable sector? We are not the junior members with business and government; we are the indispensable partner. So how do we strengthen the leadership of the social sector? Because, as Peter says, "It is not business, it is not government, it is the social sector that may yet save the society."

JC: I don't know if I will live to see it, but I expect in a number of decades that the Leader to Leader organization will be seen as having done more to shape the number of exceptional, effective Level 5 leaders in society than any other institution. It's a great contribution.

FH: Thank you.

JC: I have one last question for you. Frances, every time we interact, I come away tingly. The tingle is the energy and passion that you bring. The sparkle you bring to life, to work. It's infectious. You've never wavered. It's like a wellspring that never ends. What is the secret to never-ending passion and continual self-renewal?

FH: Do you see all those people out there? I get my energy from the people I work with. A third of my time is on college university campuses, a third with corporations, a third with nonprofits. And, in the middle of the thirds, a big chunk of time for the chief of staff of the United States Army and his people, and West Point. When I do this, it doesn't matter whether last week in New Zealand with business leaders, today with all of you ... the energy I get from them just pushes me forward. It's like magic. I can't describe it. I should be dead tired when I fly eighteen hours to New Zealand.

JC: You should be, but you're not!

FH: No. Because the people are so marvelous. You've talked about it. You're a learner. I'm a learner. But all over this world are people like this marvelous audience. We're all learners together. They keep pouring energy into me. So I have to go out and spend that energy that I've been given.

JC: I had a wonderful professor and mentor named John Gardner, whom you know, former secretary of health, education and welfare in the Johnson administration, who admonished me early in my career, "Mr. Collins, it appears to me that you spend way too much time trying to be interesting."

FH: That's John.

JC: Yes. "Why don't you invest more time in being interested?" And it strikes me that you are very much a role
model of that.

We are up on our time, and it has just been a gift to all of
us to have you here with us. And I imagine you and I will
continue our conversations for a very, very long time.

FH: Forever.

∞

A few weeks later I was speaking to the annual meeting of
the Military Child Education Coalition, in Kansas City. The
conference brought together nine hundred military officers
and spouses, working together to make a difference in the
welfare and education of 1,800,000 children of the military
in schools all over the world, "For the sake of the child, for
the good of the world." I attend each year, and this time I was
invited to give the keynote speech.

When it was over, there was warm applause and a long
standing ovation. I bowed, and as I turned to leave the lectern,
Patty Shinseki, the wife of General Eric Shinseki, appeared
beside me, took my elbow, and whispered "Don't move."
She thanked me for my presentation and ended her remarks
by saying, "You shine a light." That must have been a cue,
because the lights went out, leaving that large auditorium in
total darkness. Then loud music swelled up: "This little light
of mine, I'm going to let it shine ...," and nine hundred little
flashlights went on, moving in lovely circles as they shone in
the darkness.

Patty and I stood there. Speechless, all I could do was bow and bow and finally say, "Thank you from my heart." I've never had a more moving tribute. It will stay with me forever.

I keep my little flashlight on my desk, a reminder of a great thought leader and dear friend, Jim Collins, and a reminder of the evening when that wonderful group of military leaders and spouses made "Shine a Light" their own. And I think again of President Lincoln's words.

> I am not bound to win,
> But I am bound to be true.
> I am not bound to succeed,
> But I am bound to live
> Up to the light I have.

ABOUT THE AUTHOR

Frances Hesselbein is the president and CEO of the Leader to Leader Institute (formerly the Peter F. Drucker Foundation for Nonprofit Management) and its founding president. In 1998, Mrs. Hesselbein was awarded the Presidential Medal of Freedom, the highest civilian honor in the United States, by President Bill Clinton. The award recognized her leadership as CEO of Girl Scouts of the USA from 1976 to 1990, her role as the founding president of the Drucker Foundation, and her service as "a pioneer for women, volunteerism, diversity, and opportunity." President George H. W. Bush appointed her to the board of directors of the Commission on National and Community Service in August 1991, and to the Advisory Committee on the Points of Light Foundation in 1989.

In 2009, Mrs. Hesselbein was appointed the Class of 1951 Chair for the Study of Leadership at the U.S. Military Academy at West Point's Department of Behavioral Sciences and Leadership. She is the first woman and first nongraduate to serve in this chair. Also in 2009, the University of Pittsburgh initiated the Hesselbein Global Academy for Student Leadership and Civic Engagement. The Academy aims to develop a cadre of experienced, ethical leaders equipped to address critical issues throughout the world.

Mrs. Hesselbein serves on many nonprofit and corporate boards, including Mutual of America Life Insurance Company; Bright China Social Fund; American Express Philanthropy; the Graduate School of International Relations and Pacific Studies, University of California, San Diego; and the Alliance Advisory Council for the Center for Creative Leadership. She was the chairman of Volunteers of America from 2002 to 2006.

In 2008, Mrs. Hesselbein was presented with the International Leadership Association's Lifetime Achievement Award and the Tempo International Leadership Award. In the same year, she was named a Senior Leader at the U.S. Military Academy National Conference on Ethics in America. In 2007, Mrs. Hesselbein was awarded the John F. Kennedy Memorial Fellowship by Fulbright New Zealand. In 2003, she was the first recipient of the Dwight D. Eisenhower National Security Award. She was inducted into the Enterprising Women Hall of Fame at the seventh annual Enterprising Women of the Year Awards celebration. She is the recipient of twenty honorary doctoral degrees.

Mrs. Hesselbein is editor in chief of the award-winning quarterly journal *Leader to Leader*, and a coeditor of a book of the same name. She is the author of *Hesselbein on Leadership* and, with General Eric K. Shinseki, introduced *Be*Know* Do: Leadership the Army Way*. Mrs. Hesselbein is the coeditor of twenty-seven books in twenty-nine languages.

INDEX